American University

Washington, DC

Written by Ian Hosking, Alanna Schubach

Edited by the College Prowler Team

ISBN # 978-1-4274-0329-2

©Copyright 2011 College Prowler

All Rights Reserved
Printed in the U.S.A.
www.collegeprowler.com

Last updated: 3/23/2011

College Prowler®
5001 Baum Blvd.
Suite 750
Pittsburgh, PA 15213

Phone: (800) 290-2682
Fax: (800) 772-4972
E-Mail: info@collegeprowler.com
Web: www.collegeprowler.com

More than **200,000** student reviews on nearly **7,000** schools!

SEE IT ALL ON COLLEGEPROWLER.COM!

This book only offers a glimpse at our extensive coverage of one school out of thousands across the country. Visit *collegeprowler.com* to view our full library of content for FREE! Our site boasts thousands of photos and videos, interactive search tools, more reviews, and expanded content on nearly 7,000 schools.

CONNECT WITH SCHOOLS

Connect with the schools you are most interested in and discover new schools that match your interests.

FIND SCHOLARSHIPS

We give away $2,000 each month and offer personalized matches from a database of more than 3.2 million other scholarships!

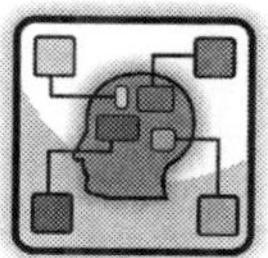

SELECT A MAJOR

We have information on every major in the country to help you choose your degree and plan your career.

USE OUR TOOLS TO HELP YOU CHOOSE

Compare schools side-by-side, estimate your chances of admission, and get personalized school recommendations.

To get started, visit <u>collegeprowler.com/register</u>

The Big Book of Colleges

Choosing the perfect school can be an overwhelming challenge. Luckily, our *Big Book of Colleges* makes that task a little less daunting. We've packed it with overviews of our full library of single-school guides—more than 400 of the nation's top schools—giving you some much-needed perspective on your search.

BIG BOOK OF COLLEGES '12
Paperback 7.75" X 10", 900+ pages
$29.95 Retail
ISBN: 978-1-4274-0326-1

To order your copy,
visit collegeprowler.com/store

How this all started...

When I was trying to find the perfect college, I used every resource that was available to me. I went online to visit school Web sites; I talked with my high school guidance counselor; I read book after book; I hired a private counselor. Sure, this was all very helpful, but nothing really told me what life was like at the schools I cared about. These sources weren't giving me enough information to be totally confident in my decision.

In all my research, there were only two ways to get the information I wanted.

The first was to physically visit the campuses and see if things were really how the brochures described them, but this was quite expensive and not always feasible. The second involved a missing ingredient: the students. Actually talking to a few students at those schools gave me a taste of the information that I needed so badly. The problem was that I wanted more but didn't have access to enough people.

In the end, I weighed my options and decided on a school that felt right and had a great academic reputation, but truth be told, the choice was still very much a crapshoot. I had done as much research as any other student, but was I 100 percent positive that I had picked the school of my dreams?

Absolutely not.

My dream in creating College Prowler was to build a resource that people can use with confidence. My own college search experience taught me the importance of gaining true insider insight; that's why the majority of this guide is composed of quotes from actual students. After all, shouldn't you hear about a school from the people who know it best?

I hope you enjoy reading this book as much as we've enjoyed putting it together. Tell me what you think when you get a chance. I'd love to hear your college selection stories.

Luke Skurman
CEO and Co-Founder
luke@collegeprowler.com

Welcome to College Prowler®

When we created College Prowler, we felt it was critical that our content was unbiased and unaffiliated with any college or university. We think it's important that our readers get honest information and a realistic impression of the student opinions on any campus—that's why if any aspect of a particular school is terrible, we (unlike a campus brochure) intend to publish it. While we do keep an eye out for the occasional extremist—the cheerleader or the cynic—we take pride in letting the students tell it like it is. We strive to create a book that's as representative as possible of each particular campus. Our books cover both the good and the bad, and whether the survey responses point to recurring trends or a variation in opinion, these sentiments are directly and proportionally expressed through our guides.

College Prowler guidebooks are in the hands of students throughout the entire process of their creation. Because you can't make student-written guides without the students, we have students at each campus who help write, randomly survey their peers, edit, layout, and perform accuracy checks on every book that we publish. From the very beginning, student writers gather the most up-to-date stats, facts, and inside information on their colleges. They fill each section with student quotes and summarize the findings in editorial reviews. In addition, each school receives a collection of letter grades (A through F) that reflect student opinion and help to represent contentment or satisfaction for each of our 20 specific categories. Just as in grade school, the higher the mark the more content or more satisfied the students are with the particular category.

Each book is the result of endless student contributions, hundreds of pages of research and writing, and countless hours of hard work. All of this has led to the creation of a student information network that stretches across the nation to every school that we cover. It's no easy accomplishment, but it's the reason that our guides are such a great resource.

When reading our books and looking at our grades, keep in mind that every college is different and that the students who make up each school are not uniform—as a result, it is important to assess schools on a case-by-case basis. Because it's impossible to summarize an entire school with a single number or description, each book provides a dialogue, not a decision, that's made up of 20 different topics and hundreds of student quotes. In the end, we hope that this guide will serve as a valuable tool in your college selection process. Enjoy!

The College Prowler Team

Table of Contents

By the Numbers

School Contact

American University
4400 Massachusetts Ave NW
Washington, DC 20016

Control:
Private Non-Profit

Academic Calendar:
Semester

Religious Affiliation:
Protestant

Founded:
1893

Web Site:
WWW.AMERICAN.EDU

Main Phone:
(202) 885-1000

Student Body

Full-Time Undergraduates:
6,404

Part-Time Undergraduates:
244

Total Male Undergraduates:
2,721

Total Female Undergraduates:
4,237

Admissions

Acceptance Rate:
53%

Total Applicants:
14,936

Total Acceptances:
7,950

Freshman Enrollment:
1,533

Yield (% of admitted students who enroll):
19%

Transfer Applications Received:
1,470

Transfer Applications Accepted:
910

Transfer Students Enrolled:
318

Transfer Application Acceptance Rate:
62%

SAT I or ACT Required?
Either

SAT I Range (25th–75th Percentile):
1750–2060

SAT I Verbal Range (25th–75th Percentile):
590–700

SAT I Math Range (25th–75th Percentile):
580–670

SAT I Writing Range (25th–75th Percentile):
580–690

ACT Composite Range (25th–75th Percentile):
26–30

ACT English Range (25th–75th Percentile):
26–32

ACT Math Range (25th–75th Percentile):
24–29

ACT Writing Range (25th–75th Percentile):
25–30

Top 10% of High School Class:
50%

Application Fee:
$60

Common Application Accepted?
Yes

Admissions Phone:
(202) 885-6000

Admissions E-Mail:
admissions@american.edu

Admissions Web Site:
admissions.american.edu/

Regular Decision Deadline:
January 15

Regular Decision Notification:
April 1

Must-Reply-By Date:
May 1

Financial Information
Out-of-State Tuition:
$34,973

Room and Board:
$12,930

Books and Supplies:
$600

Average Amount of Federal Grant Aid:
$3,420

Percentage of Students Who Received Federal Grant Aid:
10%

Average Amount of Institution Grant Aid:
$16,410

Percentage of Students Who Received Institution Grant Aid:
59%

Average Amount of State Grant Aid:
$792

Percentage of Students Who Received State Grant Aid:
6%

Average Amount of Student Loans:
$10,724

Percentage of Students Who Received Student Loans:
52%

Total Need-Based Package:
$24,294

Percentage of Students Who Received Any Aid:
82%

Financial Aid Forms Deadline:
February 15

Financial Aid Phone:
(202) 885-6100

Financial Aid E-Mail:
financialaid@american.edu

Financial Aid Web Site:
admissions.american. edu/public/contentPage/ contentPage.asp?navID=21& docID=63

Academics

The Lowdown On...
Academics

Degrees Awarded
Associate degree
Bachelor's degree
Certificate
Master's degree
Post-bachelor's certificate

Most Popular Majors
Business Administration and
Management
International Relations and
National Security Studies
Law
Political Science and
Government, General

Majors Offered
Arts
Biological Sciences
Business
Communications
Computer and Sciences
Education
Environmental Sciences
Health Care
Languages and Literature
Law
Mathematics & Statistics
Philosophy and Religion
Physical Sciences
Protective Services

Psychology & Counseling
Recreation & Fitness
Social Sciences & Liberal Arts
Social Services

Undergraduate Schools/Divisions

College of Arts and Sciences
Kogod School of Business
School of Communication
School of International
Service
School of Public Affairs

Full-Time Instructional Faculty

637

Part-Time Instructional Faculty

549

Faculty with Terminal Degree

94%

Average Faculty Salary

$92,404

Student-Faculty Ratio

13:1

Class Sizes

Fewer than 20 students: 46%
20 to 49 students: 51%
50 or more students: 3%

Full-Time Retention Rate

88%

Part-Time Retention Rate

50%

Graduation Rate

76%

Remedial Services?

No

Academic/Career Counseling?

Yes

Instructional Programs

Occupational: No
Academic: Yes
Continuing Professional: No
Recreational/Avocational: No
Adult Basic Remedial: No
Secondary (High School): No

Special Credit Opportunities

Advanced Placement (AP)
Credits: No
Dual Credit: Yes
Life Experience Credits: No

Special Study Options

Distance learning
opportunities

Study abroad
Teacher certification (below
the postsecondary level)
Weekend/evening college

Best Places to Study
Amphitheatre
Bender Library
Residence Hall Lounges

Did You Know?

The most highly-populated school is the College of Arts and Sciences.

AU is a member of the Consortium of Universities of the Washington Metropolitan Area, allowing students to enroll in courses offered by other member institutions and students at other member institutions to enroll in courses at AU.

Founded in 1893 by an Act of Congress, AU is one of only two schools in the country to bear the Congressional Seal on its diplomas.

Q A Great Choice!

Political Science and International Studies are the two most common majors at American University, and as such the programs for both majors have attracted excellent professors and offer a variety of classes to allow for specialization and an impressive breadth and depth of education. The workload varies greatly depending on the specific classes being taken and the professor teaching the class, but generally the workload is not unmanageable and it is possible to take advantage of a variety of extracurricular and employment opportunities while also maintaining a high GPA. In terms of internship and employment opportunities, American University is superior. There are countless opportunities for on-campus employment, and AU also boasts an excellent career center, which helps students to get internships on Capital Hill, or in various NGO's, non-profits, and private companies. In addition to all of these qualities, AU is made up of beautiful white buildings and classic architecture, which makes it an even more enjoyable place to go to school. Although it's expensive, it is undoubtedly worth every penny.

Q Any Major

Au promotes that if they don't offer your major you can always create one. This is rarely done but it has been done. You will need to work closely with professors and an advisor to create your program.

Q Law/Politics/Business/Communications Only!

American excels at its strengths, and tends to disregard the rest. If you are a student pursuing anything outside of the Political Science/IR/Law, Communications, or the

Business realm, people will probably question why you attend here. Since its DC, most professors have experience in the previously said fields, and are very knowledgeable people...whether that reaches the student is another question, since some professors can lack the teaching skills required to relay that knowledge to their students.

Q Health Promotion Program

Small program, about 35 undergrads & 40 grad students. Option of 5 year combined bachelor & masters program with a choice of 5 focus areas including: Health Communication, Health Policy etc. Program is very diverse, as is field. Overall anyone interested in preventative health from behavior change to exercise physiology, highly recommended.

Q Great Professors

The SIS, SPA, and SOC are top programs in their field. Workload depends on your teachers. Facilities in most majors are state of the art -- including the brand new, green, SIS building. ENDLESS internship opportunities thanks to the large alumni base.

Q Many Gen Eds

AU requires you to take 10 classes across 5 areas of study, as well as two writing classes, and a math class. That is a lot of time not devoted to your major, but they want to make sure that what you're majoring in, is what you want to be majoring in. Registration goes by number of credits completed, with RAs getting priority registration.

Q SIS

I came to American University because it has a rigorous and well renowned International Relations program and a great study abroad program. The campus is nice, the classrooms are small and the faculty is decent.

❑ Truly Hit or Miss With Academics

Granted I have only taken mostly entry-level classes at this point, but the difficulty of each class has ranged from me having to push myself to earn a B and learn a ton to the class I had to go to twice and got an A.

The College Prowler Take On...
Academics

American University employs many professors of prominence in their fields, with many instructors also working for the government or other organizations while serving as a professor. As a result of many professors being highly involved in DC politics and organizations, students often have access to Washington insider information and experiences. Of particular note are the political science, international relations, and business programs, which all emphasize DC-specific subjects and perspectives. By taking advantage of the resources of the city, the school allows students to combine their educations with real-life experience.

Classes are generally small, with most having about 30 students, and are often discussion-based. Professors are widely regarded as very good (though there are plenty of exceptions), including the many adjunct professors who teach in addition to working in the city. Despite being a small school, AU has a great drawing power for well-known and respected faculty members. Don't be surprised to see professors being interviewed or called in for their expert opinions on the news. Students find DC to be an exciting and eye-opening city, and the school's classes reflect that. DC is a fast-paced and politically-charged town, and AU incorporates the best elements of the city into its education.

The College Prowler® Grade on

Academics: B+

A high Academics grade generally indicates that professors are knowledgeable, accessible, and genuinely interested in their students' welfare. Other determining factors include class size, how well professors communicate, and whether or not classes are engaging.

Local Atmosphere

The Lowdown On...
Local Atmosphere

City, State
Washington, DC

Setting
Large city

Distances to Nearest Major Cities
Baltimore – MD – 1 hour
New York City – NY – 4 hours
Philadelphia – PA – 3 hours

Points of Interest
Adams Morgan
Dupont Circle
Georgetown
National Mall
U Street

Shopping Centers
Crystal City
Montgomery Mall
Tyson's Corner

Major Sports Teams

D.C. United: soccer
Washington Capitals: hockey
Washington Nationals:
baseball
Washington Redskins:
football
Washington Wizards:
basketball

Movie Theaters

AMC Mazza Gallerie 7

5300 Wisconsin Ave. NW
Washington,D.C.
(202) 537-9553

AMC Theatres

50 Massachusetts Ave.
Friendship Heights
(703) 998-4262

Avalon Theatre

5612 Connecticut Ave. NW
Washington,D.C.
(202) 966-6000

Did You Know?

5 Fun Facts about Washington, D.C.:
• It's built on a swamp.
• No buildings are allowed to be built higher than the Washington Monument.
• The first election in which residents legally participated was held in 1964.
• DC itself is perfectly square, and measures 15 miles on each edge.
• It's divided into quadrants (NE, NW, SE, SW), each with a distinct flavor.

Famous People from Wahington DC:
Dave Chapelle — Actor, comedian
Alyson Hannigan — actress
Goldie Hawn — actress, Kate Hudson's mom
Marvin Gaye — R&B singer
Edward Norton — actor

Local Slang:
No specific slang—DC is very much composed of residents native to other states, both northern and southern, so there's a wide range of speech patterns here.

Local Atmosphere

◯ DC Is the Place to Be!

There are always a ton of cultural, music, film, and other types of festivals going on in the DC area, not to mention all of the monuments and museums. The student/ young adult population is a very active and important demographic in DC, and everything you could possibly need is within walking distance of a metro or bus station!

◯ AU Connects Me to DC

AU connects me to Washington, DC more deeply than I would be if I just lived here on my own, or attended another area school. My professors are all plugged into the city, writing for think tanks or advising on the Hill or speaking on NPR and WAMU. I have had 3 internships in 3 years, and got credit for all 3 through AU - partly thanks to the AMAZING Career Center, especially David Fletcher, an adviser for International Studies undergrads. I have attended Supreme Court arguments, House briefings, Senate floor speeches, lectures at think tanks, and meetings with corporate giants, Ambassadors, and military rising stars. Many of those were recommended by professors as a way to see our class discussion topics play out in real time. Of course, it's not all academic and career-focused for AU students. I love all the bars and clubs; there are lots of opportunities to dance or hang out whether you're over 21 or not. My friends and I usually go to Clyde's on Thursdays - it's only 1 metro stop away and basically serves as an AU satellite campus that night. When I was underage, I usually hit Apex, a friendly gay club with a college night that's great for anybody who just wants to dance, gay or straight. Their practice of getting creative with their underage hand-stamps, choosing other letters like "H" or "A" instead of "X," makes it clear on Friday morning who you missed last night. Chef Geoff's happy hour specials are our Friday night pre-game, since it's so close and the bar has a classy vibe. Regarding the much-touted Embassy parties, a lot of people love hopping onto Swiss or Israeli territory for the evening, though that's not really my scene. My roommate, a graphic design major, always knows what's going on for First Night, so she'll take us out to Dupont for the free small-gallery shows with complimentary wine and cheese. After a late night on U street or in Dupont (both far more fun and less touristy than Adams Morgan and Georgetown, imho), I love getting late-night pizza, chili, ice cream or cupcakes from one of the famous DC spots - or, even better, the lesser-known shops that aren't as crowded. My favorite post-club fix: Mr. Yogato. Oh my God, it's delicious, and the store itself is worth the visit: whiteboards proclaim the different ways to earn discounts, including letting staff stamp your forehead with their logo or solving word puzzles, and classic video games and Connect 4 litter the tables.Students are a huge part of DC's population, and relationships with the community are getting better all the time. My roommate tutors kids in Anacostia through the FLY program, and has such a bond with her students. This year, an AU student was elected to our local ANC, representing both student and local interests in DC government. The library (where I work part-time) gives local residents access to its resources. A hall-mate freshman year was on quest to only eat free food on weekends, hopping around to various DC events at churches, on the Hill, and anywhere else. I never found out it he managed it, though...

Q **Great Atmosphere**

DC was tied for number one as the top town kids go to after they graduate college. There is always something to see and do. Free concerts at the Kennedy Center, the Smithsonians, Clubs, free showings of movies, etc. As long as you're smart about it it's a really safe place, just don't go anywhere late at night by yourself. Great shopping at Pentagon City, or Eastern Market if you want a less traditional shopping experience. It's easy to see sports at

the Verizon Center, or Nationals Stadium -- and they have
$5 game day tickets -- even if the Nationals aren't very
good. The locals hate tourists, not students: so as long
as you stand on the right and walk on the left on metro
escalators, you should be fine with locals.

Q Early-Night College Love

DC is one of the best hidden college towns around, and
American is nicely settled on the border between the city
itself and surburbia. Its only a quick school shuttle ride
to the nearest metro station, and you have downtown
DC at your fingertips! Although, DC is a pretty early city,
with most delivery places closing at 10...so stock up on
munchies for finals, since the only places open at 1am will
be Pizza Hut.

Q Fantastic

The local atmosphere has many striking similarities to that
of a utopia. It is in a fantastic, affluent area but only a short
bus ride from the hustle and bustle that is Washington D.C.
There is also Georgetown, tenelytown, and Arlington so
you can't possibly run out of fun things to do.

Q Great Cultural Events

D.C. is one of the most cultural cities in this country. The
Mall is the best place to visit and get contact with a bunch
of free Museums that bring you an excellent opportunity
to know about history, science, astrology and many others
topics. American University is located in the heart of D.C.
allowing their student to visit the mall every single week
end.

Q Friendly College Town

There is plenty to do in the area being in DC. However
there is not much immediately next to AU. It's to be set in
the suburbs. It makes you feel like you are at home.

 Pretty Cool

American University is a pretty cool place to be in terms of
the kind of places to party and museums. The location of
the metro station is also very useful for students to explore
D.C.

The College Prowler Take On...
Local Atmosphere

American University is in the northwest quadrant of DC, which, though pretty, doesn't necessarily reflect the fast-paced and urban environment of the city. Fear not—there's truly something for everyone. From the downtown area that is home to every government building imaginable, to the colorful Adams Morgan and Dupont Circle, to the neighborhoods in Southeast that some choose to mistakenly avoid, the city offers clubs, culture, and politics to all those seeking excitement and willing to explore.

DC is considered one of the best college towns in the country, and there is no shortage of young people out to have a great time (or climb the social ladder in hopes of political success). At the same time, AU offers a haven from the intensity in its quiet suburban-type setting, with easy access to I-95 and quainter towns in Maryland and Virginia.

The College Prowler® Grade on

Local Atmosphere: A

A high Local Atmosphere grade indicates that the area surrounding campus is safe and scenic. Other factors include nearby attractions, proximity to other schools, and the town's attitude toward students.

Health & Safety

The Lowdown On...
Health & Safety

Security Office
Public Safety
4400 Massachusetts Ave. NW
(202) 885-3636 (emergency);
(202) 885-2525 (non-emergency)
www.american.edu/finance/publicsafety/

Safety Services
Access control
Americard
Blue-light phones
Crime alerts
Educational programs

Escorts
Rape Aggression Defense
(RAD) Systems
Safe ride to campus

Crimes on Campus
Aggravated Assault: 2
Arson: 2
Burglary: 43
Murder/Manslaughter: 0
Robbery: 0
Sex Offenses: 0
Vehicle Theft: 1

Health Center
Student Health Center
McCable Hall, 1st floor
(202) 885-3380
*www.american.edu/ocl/
healthcenter*
Monday–Friday 9 a.m.–5
p.m.

Health Services
Counseling
Health education programs
Immunizations
Primary care medical services
Wellness center

Day Care Services?
Yes

Did You Know?

AU offers its own health insurance to students.

Sibley Hospital is always available to students in an emergency. They are staffed 24 hours a day, 7 days a week, and the ER can be reached at (202) 537-4080.

Students Speak Out On...
Health & Safety

○ Very Safe

You won't be targeted unless you make yourself a target. Also I'm a big dude who is probably intimidating to many

○ No Need for the Popo's

I have never felt unsafe on our campus. Campus police are constantly patrolling around which gets annoying sometimes, but then I think about what the big cause if really for. The blue light system is readily available if a problem should arise. The school also offers a R.A.D. System program which has different courses set up for males, females, and staff. I would definitely recommend taking the class because it teaches you self-defense in the case of an emergency.

○ It's Pretty Safe

However, just don't walk alone late at night.

○ Health and Safety Are Second Too None

Early in the school year I came down with Swine Flu. I walked right in to the Health center and with in ten minutes I was being examined by the doctor. The only negative is that you have to pay a cash co-payment, no matter what you came in for.

○ Common Sense = Pretty Safe

You can take a cab back to campus and get a voucher that pays for it. You can call for an escort at any time.

Q **Be Smart, and You'll Be Fine.**

It's when I'm out late at night that I realize AU is totally removed from that traditional city-feel. I've walked back from late nights on campus at 2 or 3 AM, and it's nearly empty, but there are always a few students around (it also helps that most of us live in the same apartment complexes, so you'll end up walking close together). I've heard the horror stories of course (walking from Tenley to campus alone is NOT the brightest idea at night), but if you use your judgment and walk in groups when you can, it'll be okay.

Q **Well, Homeland Security IS Across the Street...**

AU is a safe campus in a upper middle class neighborhood. Public Safety officers often wander around and we always joke about having Homeland Security across the street.

Q The security on campus is really good. Public Safety is always there when you need them. Since it's a small campus, there are always people around.

The College Prowler Take On...
Health & Safety

Being in a more affluent neighborhood means a lower risk for crime at AU. The campus police are visible and effective, providing students with a strong sense of comfort and security. There are blue-light phones available throughout campus in case of emergencies, and security responds quickly and effectively to crises.

In fact, many students think the campus police may be stricter and more vigilant at AU than at other schools because of a lack of serious incidents for them to attend to. In addition, being literally around the block from the Department of Homeland Security and the Japanese and Swedish embassies means the cops are not only looking out for students, but Uncle Sam is as well.

The College Prowler® Grade on

Health & Safety: B

A high grade in Health & Safety means that students generally feel safe, campus police are visible, blue-light phones and escort services are readily available, and safety precautions are not overly necessary.

Computers

The Lowdown On...
Computers

Wireless Access
Yes: Available in certain locations.

24-Hour Labs?
Yes: The Anderson Computer Lab Sunday–Friday (it closes at midnight on Saturday and reopens Sunday at 8 a.m.)

Charged to Print?
Yes: Students are allotted $25 a semester for printing, at 10 cents a page. If you go over that amount, you'll have to pay with Eagle Bucks.

Special Software & Hardware Discounts
Microsoft Office

A campus-wide map of all AU's computing facilities is available at www.library.american. edu/about/labs.html.

Lecture halls have outlets for laptops if you want to type your notes.

The Campus IT department provides software free to students, such as antivirus and writing programs.

AU offers many classes online via virtual classrooms.

Computers

Computers Are Great

there are a lot of labs to choose from, and the computers range from basic computing (internet, microsoft word) to adobe suite programs, final cut, business school labs, etc. Its not hard to find an empty computer if you need one. Almost everyone does have their own laptop, though.

Crowded but Decent.

AU definitely makes an effort to keep up with technology and demand. Basically all students have their own computers, but when mine was out of commission for 4 weeks, I found it totally practical to use ones on campus. The library is most crowded, but has the most stations, and is open 24 hours. The Kogod FSIT lab is gorgeous, and the labs in Ward are usually empty if they aren't being used for classes. You don't need your own printer: AU gives everyone a $25 subsidy (more than enough, now that the library prints double-sides) per semester, and the printer locations are usable and located in smart places.

NEEDS MORE

There needs to be more computers since it gets crowded especially during final times. They also need to make more laptops available.

Overall Decent Access

There is a computer lab under the south side dorms which doesn't get much traffic, but the computers at the library are the best for pulling all-nighters. The library also lends out laptops that you can take with you around campus, just beware of late fees. The campus is totally wireless but the connectivity can be pretty unreliable, especially in the dorms. I recommend an ethernet cable so you never have to worry about getting kicked offline. You get $25 a semester in printing bucks for the printers in the labs and in the library so you don't really need a printer but a laptop is a MUST. Some classes even require one.

Q Bring a Laptop, but Not a Printer

I know there are computer labs in the Library (several, including a Media lab), SIS, Anderson Hall, Hurst (stocked with math/stats/science software and tutors on standby), Kogod (business/finance/stats software), Tenley Campus/ Federal Hall, and Katzen Arts Center (design/film/art software), and one other that I can't remember. There are also a dozen public computers scattered through the other buildings, including MGC (the student center). All the main labs have printers available. The library printers, especially on the ground floor, are crazy busy during the break between classes, so don't wait until the last minute to print your assignment.Having a laptop definitely helps, unless you want to camp out at one of the labs for all your homework. If you live in one of the dorms with their own labs (Anderson/Letts/Centennial, Federal), it might be easier for those who don't want to buy one. Most are 24-hours a day during the workweek, if you do want to go that route. The library also rents out laptops, but never for more than a day. Also available for rent are DVD players, software, headphones, film equipment, etc. EagleNet, the campus wireless, is very secure, but occasionally slow - especially when everyone is streaming something at once, like the SuperBowl or the health care vote in the House. PC users sometimes have to wait a while for Cisco to let them log in, when they are booting up and connecting; Mac users never do. PCs and Macs can get repairs and service from staff in the Anderson lab, and if your machine is too broken to be saved, BestBuy is right across from the AU Shuttle stop in Tenleytown.

Q **Not Enough Printers!**
$25/semester of printing money included in tuition, not enough printers, decent number of computers. Tough to find space during finals, but otherwise good space to work.

Q **Eaglenet Is Horrible.**
They boast a wireless campus but often its very slow or not working altogether.

Q Labs are not crowded. Everyone has a laptop—it's great to have one. I recommend it.

The College Prowler Take On...
Computers

The super-fast Ethernet connection at AU has students wondering why they ever tolerated the trials of dial-up connections. The wireless network is a great convenience for students with laptops who want to emerge from their dorm rooms when writing term papers. This makes buying a laptop the best choice for those bringing their own computers.

Bringing your own computer would be best, but students who can't bring one need not worry; there are plenty of computer labs on campus with Internet access, but some tend to get crowded, so it pays to acquaint yourself with the ones that don't fill up quickly.

The College Prowler® Grade on

Computers: B-

A high grade in Computers designates that computer labs are available, the computer network is easily accessible, and the campus's computing technology is up-to-date.

Facilities

The Lowdown On...
Facilities

Campus Size
84 acres

Student Centers
Mary Graydon Center

Main Libraries
American University Library
AU Media Services
AU Music Library
AU Washington College of
Law Library
Seminary Library
Wesley Theological

Service & Maintenance Staff
71

Popular Places to Chill
Amphitheatre
Mary Graydon Center
The Quad

Bar on Campus
None

Bowling on Campus
None

Coffeehouse on Campus
Megabytes Cafe underneath the Tunnel
Pura Vida Fair Trade Coffee in Mary Graydon Center
The Davenport in the School of International Service

Movie Theater on Campus
None

Favorite Things To Do
Political speakers are popular on campus, and various clubs
host impressive guests almost weekly. Recent speakers include
President Barack Obama, Former Speaker of the House Newt
Gingrich, Bolivian President Evo Morales, and Congressman
Ron Paul. When students aren't attending the numerous
political events, they can hang out on the quad for cookouts
or Frisbee games, workout in Bender Fitness Center, watch
AU's Division I basketball team, and play intramural sports on
the fields.
Students can see shows and recitals at Katzen Art Center and
Greenberg Theatre, or watch movies, television, and concerts
in the Tavern. Bender Arena hosts sports games, including
Division I basketball, while the Kennedy Political Union brings
a large number of prominent speakers to campus.

Facilities

Q General Overview

Library- The library is great, it's open 24/7 and the faculty working in the library is really helpful.Faculty- Professors, student advisors, and faculty members are really driven to help students succeed. There are so many different ways the faculty reaches out to help students from homework help centers, to math labs, to the availability when it comes to professors through office hours or emailing them. Activities- It's really easy to become involved with clubs and things like that, the student population is really friendly. Aesthetics- the campus is really beautiful, the buildings are so pretty and it's nice to walk through. The location is perfect and safe, and it's so nice to be able to have a campus in the middle of the city.Residence Halls- The dorms aren't amazing, but there's tons of space for storage, they're really safe, they are all connected and people on the floor are friendly. The bathrooms are always clean and there's a kitchenette on every floor complete with stoves, so it's easy to cook.

Q Very Easy to Find

Everything is very easy to find. Simply consult either a campus map or employee and they would be more than happy to help you.

Q Campus Aesthetics

Campus is tiny but beautiful. There's no more than a ten minute walk to any class, but the quad is a beautiful green space and there are always, always flowers.

Q **Generally Well-Thought Out.**

AU works to maintain shiny-looking spaces to entice prospective students. As a student who lives off-campus but spends the majority of the day on-campus studying or in class, there are always places to study and hang out: Mary Graydon is nicely quiet in the mornings, and loud and people-filled in the afternoons/early evenings, and the small cyber lounge area is nice. Kogod has the best lounges, but the Batelle atrium is nice, and Katzen is nicely empty most of the time. The library is one of the most unattractive buildings you'll see, but they make an effort to have as many couches, tables, etc. available as possible. Jacobs Fitness Center is weirdly designed and the upstairs cardio machines fill up during busy times, but it's clean. Student Activities can be a real pain, but once you've gotten to know them in the context of your student organization, it's fairly simple to reserve spaces across campus for meetings and activities.

Q **Facilites Are Adequate**

American University's facilities serve their purpose. Nothing is run down, while nothing stands out as being too new. American's student union and gym have everything a student can need, but not everything a student wants.

Q **Depends on the Building**

The facilities at American vary. Most of the classrooms and other student centers have been updated and look pretty nice and feel clean and new, but some, especially the residence halls haven't been updated and you can definitely tell. But even the building that haven't been updated aren't terrible. They just aren't as nice as the other buildings.

Q **Student center is good, library is awful**

The student center is pretty good and a great place to hang out. The library is awful for the size and prestige of the University, and I study at the Washington School of Law library every chance I get because of how much better it is. Campus is an oasis in DC, but doesn't look like Hogwarts by any stretch.

Q   The facilities are fine. I'm not blown away by any of them, but they all certainly meet my needs. AU doesn't have tons of money, so they don't have flashy facilities, but like I said, they always get the job done for me.

The College Prowler Take On...
Facilities

AU has taken great pains in the past to update and modernize its facilities, but students remain underwhelmed due to the facilities' small sizes. However, most agree that they are good enough, with Internet access and a decent choice in food. Students generally approve of the dorms, and the fitness center is a popular spot and usually crowded with the health-conscious population.

Facilities at AU may not be thrilling, but they are always clean and up-to-date. Students are far more active outside the confines of campus and in the city around them, which contributes to AU's less animated campus life compared to other universities.

The College Prowler® Grade on
Facilities: B-

A high Facilities grade indicates that the campus is aesthetically pleasing and well-maintained; facilities are state-of-the-art, and libraries are exceptional. Other determining factors include the quality of both athletic and student centers and an abundance of things to do on campus.

Campus Dining

The Lowdown On...
Campus Dining

Average Meal Plan Cost
$4300 per year

Freshman Meal Plan Required?
Yes: Freshmen must purchase meal plans of at least 150 blocks, with 200 block and unlimited block meal plans also available.

24-Hour Dining
None

Dining Halls & Campus Restaurants

Block Express
Location: Mary Graydon Center
Food: Boxed lunches to go
Hours: Monday–Thursday 9 a.m.–8 p.m., Friday 9 a.m.–3 p.m.

Chick-fil-A
Location: Mary Graydon Center
Food: Chicken, fast food
Hours: Monday–Thursday 11 a.m.–11 p.m., Friday 11 a.m.–6 p.m.

Eagle's Nest
Location: Butler Pavilion
Food: Convenience store food
Hours: Monday–Friday 7 a.m.–2 a.m., Saturday–Sunday 10 a.m.–2 a.m.

Einstein Bros.
Location: Mary Graydon Center
Food: Bagels, muffins, coffee
Hours: Monday–Thursday 7:30 a.m.–6 p.m., Friday 7:30 a.m.–3 p.m.

Field of Greens
Location: Mary Graydon Center
Food: Tossed-to-order salads
Hours: Monday–Thursday 11 a.m.–8 p.m., Friday 11 a.m.–3 p.m.

McDonald's
Location: Butler Pavilion
Food: Fast food
Hours: Monday–Saturday 6 a.m.–11 p.m., Sunday 7 a.m.–11 p.m.

Megabytes Café
Location: Under the tunnel
Food: Salads, sandwiches, ice cream, curry, Starbucks coffee
Hours: Monday–Friday 8 a.m.–8 p.m., Saturday–Sunday 10 a.m.–6 p.m.

Panini Express
Location: Mary Graydon Center
Food: Grilled-to-order sandwiches
Hours: Monday–Thursday 11 a.m.–8 p.m., Friday 11 a.m.–3 p.m.

Pura Vida
Location: Mary Graydon Center
Food: Espresso, latte
Hours: Monday–Thursday 7:30 a.m.–9 p.m., Friday 7:30 a.m.–6 p.m.

Subway
Location: In the Eagle's Nest
Food: Subs and salads
Hours: Daily 10 a.m.–2 a.m.

Tavern
Location: Mary Graydon
Center, first floor
Food: Pizza, burgers, and
beer
Hours: Monday–Thursday
11 a.m.–11 p.m., Friday
11 a.m.–6 p.m., Sunday 4
p.m.–11 p.m.

Terrace Dining Room (TDR)
Location: Mary Graydon
Center, bottom floor
Food: All you care to eat
comfort food, salads, deli,
vegetarian, ice cream,
international cuisines
Hours: Monday–Friday
8 a.m.–9 p.m.,
Saturday–Sunday 11 a.m.–3
p.m., 5 p.m.–7:30 p.m.

Wagshal's American Café
Location: Ward Circle
Building
Food: American
Hours: Monday–Thursday 7
a.m.–10 p.m., Friday 7 a.m.–5
p.m., Saturday 8 a.m.–4 p.m.

The comment board in TDR offers some of the best-hidden comedy. Make sure to check out students' complaints, and staffers' responses, before you go back to your dorm.

AU is ranked as the #1 school for vegetarians in the nation by PETA.

Campus Dining

Q Food

Excellent food and consideration for vegetarians/vegans

Q Terrace Dining Room

It's the only dining hall on campus. It's...alright. Sometimes, the food is pretty good. There are tons of options from pizza to asian food to cheeseburgers. However, there are a lot of nights that you go and the food is just not as good as other nights. Those nights, you go to the Eagle's Nest and pick up something to make yourself or to snack on.

Q Better Than Average

There's only one dining hall which means that everyone gets sick of TDR at some point. They consistently have decent food and they always have salad stations, sandwich stations and cereal. There's a lot of food but it's only so good.

Q Average

The dining at AU itself is average. However, the meal plan is terrible. At least a 150 block plan for freshman and those 150 meal plans can only go to three locations. The cash with our meal plans (Eaglebucks) can be used on campus and at local businesses; definitely a plus.

Q Glad to Be Done With It.

I find on-campus dining to be pretty lacking on AU's campus, but that might be because our off-campus options are so much better comparatively. I spent 1.5 years on a meal plan (200, 150, then 75), and it was fine if you could look past the price/meal (something like $13 or $14). TDR has decent, not stellar selection, and the staff can range from sweet to really off-putting. Tavern is awful. During the day, you can find a decent sandwich in Ward, but a lot of the time, you end up stuck with Subway, McDonald's and the Eagle's Nest.

Q Fair Quality but High Price

The school dining hall has an excellent variety of quality food including vegetarian options that are always available. However, the cost is high and it is not open for long hours on weekends. The school offers few other places on campus that accepts either the school meal swipes or the flex dollar. There are a couple of places that I think have good food at a comparatively reasonable price, but I wish there were a greater variety of vendors that offer more reasonably priced food.

Q

I personally think that the food is fantastic, especially for a college dining hall. There is a ton of variety, and they use very fresh ingredients. Burgers and stir-fry is made to order, and it's all pretty tasty. We have a pay place called the Marketplace, which is where a lot of people hang out during the day. It is all pretty good.

Q

To be honest, the food on campus is pretty bad. The cafeteria lacks a wide selection of food. Also, in the supposed campus effort to fight Global Warming, the administration has cut back greatly on meat. Worst of all, it is nearly impossible to maintain any sort of strict diet, while only eating on campus.

The College Prowler Take On...
Campus Dining

AU's cafeteria is considered much better than typical college fare, featuring unusual multiethnic cuisine and vegetarian and vegan options that are usually very tasty. Students complain more about getting bored with food from the same source throughout their semesters, rather than the quality of the food.

There are other options for those seeking variety—AU has several fast food options, as well as an on-campus convenience store (Eagle's Nest). Students who can afford to fork over a few dollars will do well to venture off campus and try some of DC's many restaurants.

The College Prowler® Grade on

Campus Dining: B

The grade on Campus Dining addresses the quality of both school-owned dining halls and independent on-campus restaurants as well as the price, availability, and variety of food.

Off-Campus Dining

The Lowdown On...
Off-Campus Dining

Restaurant Listings

Z-Burger
Food: Burgers
4321 Wisconsin Ave. NW
202-966-1999
www.goodstuffeatery.com
Price: $3-$7

Afterwords Café
Food: Sandwiches, salads, dessert
1517 Connecticut Ave., NW
(202) 387-1462
www.kramers.com/www/Cafémain.htm

Price: $4-$15
Cool Features: Attached to Kramerbooks, a popular independent bookstore in Dupont Circle. Open late!

American City Movie Diner
Food: Typical diner food
5532 Connecticut Ave., NW
(202) 244-1949
www.americancitydiner.com
Price: $10-$15
Cool Features: Retro '50s atmosphere, special dining

room where old movies
are screened on an 8-by-8
screen.

Angelico Pizzeria
Food: Pizza, salads,
sandwiches
4529 Wisconsin Ave., NW
202-243-3030
www.angelicopizzeria.com
Price: $3-$10

Armand's Chicago-Style Pizza
Food: Famous deep Dish
pizza or traditional style,
wings, salad, subs
1140 19th St. NW #200
(202) 331-9500
www.armandspizza.com
Price: $5-$10
Cool Features: Fast delivery.

Buca di Beppo
Food: Italian
1825 Connecticut Ave., NW
(202) 232-8466
www.bucadibeppo.com
Price: $15-$20
Cool Features: Family-sized
portions, wacky old
photographs and artwork on
the walls.

Chef Geoff's
Food: Gourmet
3201 New Mexico Ave., NW
(202) 237-7800
www.chefgeoff.com
Price: $25-$35

Cool Features: Live jazz band
during Sunday brunch every
week.

Chipotle
Food: Mexican
1837 M St., NW
(202) 466-4104
www.chipolte.com
Price: $7-$12
Cool Features: Very fresh
ingredients.

Equinox Restaurant
Food: Fine dining
818 Connecticut Ave. NW
202-331-8118
www.equinoxrestaurant.com
Price: $25-$50

Guapo's
Food: Mexican
4515 Washington Ave. NW
(202) 686-3588
Price: $10-$20
Cool Features: Known for
their margaritas and fajitas.

IHOP
Food: Breakfast, pancakes
1523 Alabama Ave. SE
202-563-5890
www.ihop.com
Price: $7-$12

Lebanese Taverna
Food: Lebanese/Middle
Eastern
2641 Connecticut Ave. NW
(202) 265-8681
*www.lebanesetaverna.com/
restaurants/dc*

Price: $12-$25
Cool Features: In fashionable Woodley Park.

Manny & Olga's Pizza

Food: Gyros, pizza, salads, subs, wings
1641 Wisconsin Ave. NW
202-337-1000
www.mannyandolgas.com
Price: $6-$13

Mayflower Chinese

Food: Chinese
4427 Wisconsin Ave. NW
(202) 299-9502
Price: $5-$10

Neisha Thai Restaurant

Food: Thai cuisine
4445 Wisconsin Ave. NW
202 966-7088
www.neisha.net
Price: $6-$15

Old Ebbitt Grill

Food: American
675 15 St. NW
(202) 347-4800
www.ebbitt.com
Price: $15-$30
Cool Features: Best burgers in town.

Osman & Joe's Steak 'n Eggs Kitchen

Food: Breakfast, burgers, sandwiches, salads
4700 Wisconsin Ave. NW
202-686-1201
www.osmanandjoes.com/menu.html
Price: $6-$20

Philadelphia Cheesesteak Factory

Food: Burgers, cheesesteaks, hoagies, salads, wings
3347 M St.
202-333-8040
phillysteakfactory.com
Price: $5-$10

Pizza Movers

Food: Calzones, pizza
1618 Wisconsin Ave., NW
202-333-9199
www.pizzamoversonline.net
Price: $6-$20

Robeks Fruit Smoothies

Food: Salads, smoothies
4523 Wisconsin Ave., NW
202-244-1784
www.robeks.com
Price: $5-$10

Satay Club

Food: Asian, sushi
4654 Wisconsin Ave., NW
202-363-8888
www.asiansatayclub.com
Price: $7-$20

Spring Garden Restaurant

Food: Chinese
4916 Wisconsin Ave., NW
202-363-1698
www.springgardencarryout.com
Price: $5-$10

Tastee Diner

Food: American
118 Washington Blvd.,
Bethesda MD
(301) 953-7567
www.tasteediner.com
Price: $8-$12
Cool Features: Breakfast
served 24 hours a day.

Tono Sushi

Food: Japanese
2605 Connecticut Ave., NW
(202) 332-7300
www.tonosushi.com
Price: $12-$25
Cool Features:
"Americanized" menu
options. Lunch specials daily.

Wingo's

Food: Breakfast, sandwiches,
wings
3207 O St. NW
202-338-2478
www.wingos.com
Price: $4-$10

Best Asian

Mayflower Chinese
Satay Club
Spring Garden Restaurant

Best Breakfast

IHOP
Osman & Joe's Steak 'n Eggs
Kitchen

Best Healthy

Afterwords Café
Equinox Restaurant
Robeks Fruit Smoothies
Whole Foods

Best Pizza

Angelico Pizzeria
Manny & Olga's Pizza
Philadelphia Cheesesteak
Factory
Pizza Movers

Best Wings

Pizza Movers
Wingo's

Best Place to Take Your Parents

Buca di Beppo
Neisha Thai Restaurant

24-Hour Dining

Mayflower Chinese
Osman & Joe's Steak 'n Eggs
Kitchen
Wingo's

Other Places to Check Out

Five Guys Burgers and Fries
Hawk N' Dove
Heritage Indian
Ravi Kabob
Thai Chef

Grocery Stores

Giant
5400 Westbard Ave.,
Bethesda
(301) 652-1484

Safeway Food & Drug: Washington Stores
1855 Wisconsin Ave. NW
(202) 333-3223

Trader Joe's
10741 Columbia Pike
(301) 681-1675
www.traderjoes.com

Whole Foods Market
1440 P St. NW
(202) 332-4300

Off-Campus Dining

GREAT Off-Campus Dining

DC has every type of food you could imagine, and anything you could want is just a metro ride away. There are a lot of places that are within walking distance of campus too, and there are a ton of opportunities for discounts and stuff with student ID or Blue Crew card.

A Lot of Ethnic Eestaurants

Students at American University can taste diverse ethnic tastes in Washington DC. To illustrate, there are Japanese, Thai, Korean, Mexican, and Italian restaurants near campus. These restaurants are good and students often enjoy eating out. There is always new taste that students can find in Washington DC.

Dining Options Unlimited

In DC, there are an unlimited number of options for dining. In the nearby Tenleytown, there are small American and Mexican restaurants as well as the usual chain restaurants. The Dupont and Adam's Morgan neighborhoods provide more college food outlets like pita places, hookah bars, pizza joints, etc. Georgetown has amazing ethnic restaurants as well as pricey French and American ones. You'll never be bored with eating off campus.

Tenleytown

The shuttle runs to the tenleytown metro stop that has a variety of good places to eat. You can always take the metro to a favorite of your choice, just a few minutes away.

﹒ Delicious but Expensive

There's mexican, pizza, chinese, thai, deli, Cheesecake Factory, italian, FROZEN YOGURT!,whole foods, Chipotle, Z Burger, honestly anything you can think of right in Tenleytown or Friendship Heights. Everything is pretty expensive though. If you eat out in the city at a sit-down restaurant, expect to drop $30 for one person. If you eat out in Tenleytown or Friendship Heights at a sit-down restaurant, expect to drop $15-$20 for one person. Fast food (Chipotle, Z Burger, Popeyes, etc) expect to send around $10, unless your hitting up one of the 92,349,823 McDonalds in the 2 mile radius of AU.

﹒ If You're Willing to Venture Downtown...

There's plenty of places around. Dupont, Adams Morgan, Georgetown, U St., Bethesda..but on a day-to-day basis, you'll still find yourself going to the same places around AU/Tenleytown: Chipotle, Le Pain Quotidien, Two Amy's, Cactus Cantina, occasionally Steak and Egg...they're good, but you'll be happier if you change it up occasionally.

We live in the city—your wallets gotta be pretty thick to eat off campus.

Tenleytown and the surrounding area have a good selection of places to eat. Pizza Boli's is great for pizza that isn't expensive. There is take-out Chinese, Thai, Italian, Subway, Chipotle, and a deli. Outside of Tenleytown, there are tons of places to eat in DC. Georgetown, Dupont, and Adams Morgan are all great places to eat.

The College Prowler Take On...
Off-Campus Dining

It seems that every country in the world has not only an embassy in DC but also a restaurant. The more adventurous your tastes run, the more fun you'll have exploring cuisine in the city. Be careful though, pricey menus have been known to hurt students' already notoriously thin wallets.

Fortunately for students with thin wallets, cheap eats can be had easily at the all night diners and eateries that surround campus. Students stress the importance of going beyond the comforts of fast food and late-night pizza and experiencing the endless international flavors that the city offers.

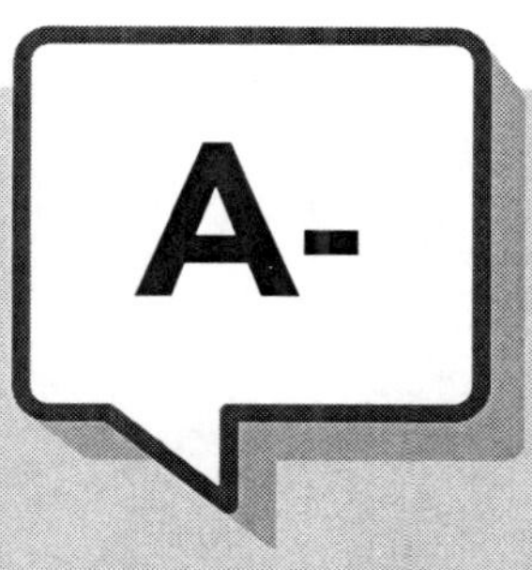

The College Prowler® Grade on

Off-Campus Dining: A-

A high Off-Campus Dining grade implies that off-campus restaurants are affordable, accessible, and worth visiting. Other factors include the variety of cuisine and the availability of alternative options (vegetarian, vegan, kosher).

Campus Housing

The Lowdown On...
Campus Housing

On-Campus Housing Available?
Yes

Number of Dormitories
10

Campus Housing Capacity
3,713

Average Housing Costs
$8,630

Dormitories

Anderson

Floors: 7
Number of Occupants: 300
Bathrooms: Single-sex communal
Coed: Yes
Residents: Freshmen and upperclassmen
Room Types: Doubles
Special Features: Houses more students than any other hall; has an Honors hall; several Greek Chapter rooms; South Side Computer lab is on bottom floor.

Capital Hill

Floors: 5
Number of Occupants: 194
Bathrooms: Single-sex communal
Coed: Yes
Residents: Freshmen and upperclassmen
Room Types: Doubles, triples
Special Features: Oldest and most ornate hall boasting wide marble staircase and high ceilings; houses the Tenley Fitness Center.

Centennial

Floors: 6
Number of Occupants: 260
Bathrooms: Semi-private
Coed: Yes
Residents: Upperclassmen
Room Types: Suites
Special Features: Only dorm reserved strictly for upperclassmen.

Congressional Hall

Floors: 3
Number of Occupants: 160
Bathrooms: Single-sex communal
Coed: Yes
Residents: Freshmen and upperclassmen
Room Types: Doubles, triples
Special Features: Staffed 24 hours a day, is where all the residents of Tenley Campus check in, and where students catch the shuttle to the main campus.

Federal Hall

Floors: 3
Number of Occupants: 105
Bathrooms: Single-sex communal
Coed: Yes
Residents: Freshmen and upperclassmen
Room Types: Doubles, triples
Special Features: Contains the mail room; cafeteria on the first floor.

Hughes

Floors: 7
Number of Occupants: 260
Bathrooms: Single-sex communal
Coed: Yes
Residents: Freshmen and upperclassmen

Room Types: Doubles, triples
Special Features: Known
for its strong sense of
community, bottom floor is
a computer cluster; houses
two Honors floors; each room
individually controls their air
conditioning and heat; TV
lounges; laundry facilities.

Leonard

Floors: 8
Number of Occupants: 280
Bathrooms: Single-sex
communal
Coed: Yes
Residents: Freshmen and
upperclassmen
Room Types: Doubles, triples
Special Features:
International/intercultural
hall, in which multiculturalism
is a primary focus; bottom
floor is a computer cluster;
each room individually
controls their air-conditioning
and heat; TV lounges;
laundry facilities.

Letts

Floors: 6
Number of Occupants: 250
Bathrooms: Single-sex
communal
Coed: Yes
Residents: Freshmen and
upperclassmen
Room Types: Doubles, triples
Special Features:
Second-largest hall; houses
the Community Service floor

and an Honors floor; South
Campus Fitness Center is
located in hall, as is the
Game and Recreation Center.

McDowell

Floors: 7
Number of Occupants: 250
Bathrooms: Single-sex
communal
Coed: Yes
Residents: Freshmen and
upperclassmen
Room Types: Singles, suites,
doubles, triples
Special Features: Houses the
North Side Fitness Center;
computer cluster on bottom
floor; each room individually
controls their air-conditioning
and heat; TV lounges;
laundry facilities; includes
community service and
wellness floors.

Nebraska

Floors: 3
Bathrooms: Private
Coed: Yes
Residents: Upperclassmen
and graduate students
Room Types: Suites
Special Features: Fully
furnished with separate
bedrooms.

Undergrads Living On Campus
75%

Best Dorms
Centennial
Leonard
Nebraska

Worst Dorms
Letts
McDowell

What You Get
Air-conditioning
Bed
Bookshelf
Desk
Heater
Plenty of closet and drawer
space

Campus Housing

Q Letts Hall 09-10

i'm a freshman in letts hall right now. i signed up for both halls on south side, considering that it's the louder, more fun side of campus. north is known for being quiet. when getting a ride to parties, mainly frat parties, they tend to meet right outside of letts and anderson, and they round people up. letts is a lot of fun, and very clean. my only complaints about the dorms is that letts is known as "the lett-o" (ghetto) compared to anderson. anderson has the nicest lounges also, why is the package system always down on south side? i don't know if it's like that on north side but it's mad annoying. living on campus is very convenient, but a little overpriced.

Q Good but Not Great.

Most student move off campus after two years. This is generally because it is very easy to get caught breaking the rules (ex. drinking) in the dorms, because living off campus is cheaper, and because it is very tough to get the room you want as a sophomore.

Q North Side Vs South Side

On-campus housing for AU is split into North Side and South Side, with each having its own benefits and draw backs. North Side is much quieter, no fire alarms, and you might actually get some studying done in your dorm. South Side is where the social center is on campus, and you don't miss a thing, but it's the part of campus that never sleeps.

ℚ It Really Depends

If you're an upperclassman, good luck. AU basically houses only 25% of juniors and seniors right now, but they are planing to build a lot more housing, so that will change in a few years. The south side if campus has pretty good dorms, but the north side ones are kind of gross.

ℚ Only Been There for One Year

The dorms are nice overall, but too cramped when they're being used for triples. McDowell also has some problems with mold on some floors. The cost is a bit high, but the campus is beautiful and there's a lot to do in the city. The food is only so-so, and sometimes makes people sick.

ℚ Great for Underclassmen

Dorms tend to be on the larger side (compared to other schools), clean and centrally located to classes. Centennial and Anderson Halls are regarded as the most widely desired. Especially with the Perch on the first floor of Anderson.However, housing in DC is expensive and Room and Board cost reflects that. Room selection is awful, and Housing and Dining are completely unresponsive to civil requests. Plus, housing is no longer guarunteed for upperclassmen.

ℚ

All the rooms are the same, and they're all pretty nice, though a little on the small side. We have two sides, north and south. The south side is a lot crazier and a lot more fun, but it is also a little dirtier. I would still recommend living in Anderson, though; you'll have a blast. Avoid Letts; it's kind of dingy, but it's still fun. On the north side is Hughes (avoid this one at all costs; it's very boring), McDowell (it's nice, but quiet and has lots of athletes), and Leonard (it's the international dorm and actually a lot of fun, with really interesting people). Live in Leonard if you want to have a different experience.

Dorms are relatively nice and are cleaned by a service almost everyday. It's nice that we have a kitchen on every floor, and it's cleaned for us. Just remember that north side (Leonard, Hughes, and McDowell) are considered the quieter dorms, but are by no means boring. Leonard is the international hall, but you don't have to be an international student to live there. Many of my friends have great experiences there. South side tends to be a bit rowdier, with many of the sororitiy sisters and frat brothers occupying the rooms. But be warned—the fire alarms will go off . . . and during rush . . . all the time . . . 2 p.m., 2 a.m. . . . all the time.

The College Prowler Take On...
Campus Housing

AU dorms cater to students of varied dispositions. The north side dorms of Hughes, McDowell, and Leonard are considered quieter, but residents there say they have tight-knit communities because they are smaller. The south side dorms, Letts, Anderson, and Centennial, are home to more frat brothers and sorority sisters, and are therefore a little rowdier.

Leonard is home to the school's many international students, and there are specialized floors elsewhere, including all-women floors and community service floors. Honors floors and Learning Community floors, where students live with similarly interested roommates, are becoming increasingly popular. Most students are satisfied with housing options, as long as they live somewhere appropriate to their personalities. Many freshmen live on campus and say it makes meeting people easier, but by junior year, students start moving off campus.

The College Prowler® Grade on

Campus Housing: B+

A high Campus Housing grade indicates that dorms are clean, well-maintained, and spacious. Other determining factors include variety of dorms, proximity to classes, and social atmosphere.

Off-Campus Housing

The Lowdown On...
Off-Campus Housing

Undergrads Living Off Campus
25%

Average Off-Campus Room & Board
$12,930

Average Rents
1 BR: $1,100
2 BR: $1,500
4 BR: $2,900
Studio: $800

Best Time to Look for a Place
At least two months in advance, though the best apartment buildings fill up fast.

Popular Areas
Bethesda
Friendship Heights
Tenleytown

Off-Campus Housing

Q What I Have Heard

Although I have never had the chance to live off campus. I have only heard great and wondrous things from the people that have.

Q Cheaper Than on Campus

Housing is expensive but it's cheaper than staying on campus

Q No Flexibility for Commuters

There is a website with options to students on how to get apartments near the university but there is not a dedicated service for this and it SHOULD specially for out of town and relocated students. DC is extremely expensive so I commute from NoVa. The commute can get very bad.

Q Many but Expensive

I am looking for apartments right now. Around campus things are pretty pricey, and I have seen a lot of rip-offs like "a move-in fee that's only $400!". Otherwise though, there are a lot of complexes in the area.

Q Appartments Are Okay

There are a lot of off-campus housing near American University. However, it is expensive to live by oneself. The high cost is understandable because there are located in Washington DC. Therefore, many students share a room with friends. It is convenient because it only takes 5 to 10 minutes to go to the university on foot.

Q Got Bank?

There aren't many choices for off-campus housing. Since American University is in the heart of Washington D.C., the prices are fairly steep for what they have to offer. Two of the closer apartments are The Berkshire and Greenbriar. These two just happen to be right next to each other and average at about $4500 per month. Unfortunately, the landlords charge you for every additional person over 3 that stays in the room. The walk to the campus from these two popular apartment complexes is about 3 blocks.

Q Expensive and a Parking Nightmare

DC is just a pricey town to live in, and there aren't that many low cost options for students nearby because AU is in a very rich neighborhood. Parking is just a nightmare city wide, but combining city parking restrictions with AU parking restrictions and it gets confusing and costly in a hurry.

Q Good

Availability, convenience,cost,landlords,parking,safety is very fine

Off-Campus Housing

Finding suitable and affordable off-campus housing in a decent neighborhood can be a huge headache for students, and they often find they must have one or more roommates to swing an apartment or house. Despite this, a significant amount of upperclassmen choose to leave campus. One pro to off-campus life is that in DC, you're never too far from a Metro, so you can find your way to AU for classes quite easily.

Two options are the Park Bethesda and Grover-Tunlaw apartment buildings. These were previously controlled by the University as upperclassman and graduate student housing, but have since been made available for rent to the public. They are still popular among students, however.

The College Prowler® Grade on

Off-Campus Housing: B-

A high grade in Off-Campus Housing indicates that apartments are of high quality, close to campus, affordable, and easy to secure.

Diversity

The Lowdown On...
Diversity

African American
4%

Native American
0%

Asian American
5%

White
56%

Hispanic
4%

Unknown
23%

International
7%

Out-of-State Students
99%

Faculty Diversity

African American: 6%
Asian American: 7%
Hispanic: 4%
International: 3%
Native American: 0%
White: 80%
Unknown: 0%

Historically Black College/University?

No

Student Age Breakdown

Under 18: 1%
18-19: 33%
20-21: 29%
22-24: 19%
25+: 18%

Economic Status

Though AU is certainly culturally diverse, most students are upper-middle-class, with a significant population being much wealthier.

Gay Pride

Two words: very acceptive. The GLBTA Resource center takes an active role in helping AU students find GLBTA related volunteer, internship, and study abroad opportunities.

Most Common Religions

AU is affiliated with the United Methodist Church, but there is also a large Jewish population.

Political Activity

Ranked the most politically active school in the country, AU boast extremely active College Republicans, Democrats, and Libertarians, in addition to a myriad special issue groups.

Minority Clubs on Campus

South Asian Students Association, Black Student Alliance, Muslim Student Association, Latin American Students Association

Q I Don't Think You Can Get Much More Diverse

With a student body that is over 40% international students, and where the rest are from all over the United States, AU has by far one of the most diverse campuses I have ever seen. Walk through the quad and I guarantee you will hear at least 10 different languages being spoken.

Q Lots of Racial Diversity, but Everyone Is Rich

I think I've honestly met a kid from every country in the world, but I've never met a kid who wasn't able to afford AU...I mean at a school that costs well above $50,000, what else do you expect?

Q Acceptance

I would say that mostly everyone is open to other races and sexual orientations.

Q Diverse in Some Ways

everyone has a different life story, and everyone is really cultural. the one thing so many people have in common at this school is that they come from wealthy families. AU does give out a lot of financial aid, but it's still so expensive that it's hard to reach out to any other groups. there aren't many african americans either.

Q Everyone Is Welcome

There is every type of nationality here that you can think of.

Q American University Diversity

The school cost so much it's difficult to get a great deal of diversity. There are a lot of International students.

Q **International, Not Ethnic, Diversity**
Diversity at AU comes mainly from its International
Students, not from its race. When you look around campus
everyone is pretty white. Different racial groups tend to
stick together because they are such a minority.

Q AU is diverse nationally and internationally, but not
as much racially or economically. The AU administration
is hell-bent on making the school the most diverse,
international American campus in the history of the world,
which, I guess, is good. But it might be better to tune up
the academic curriculum first.

The College Prowler Take On...
Diversity

When examining diversity, it depends what one considers diverse. Religiously, AU students come from many different backgrounds. Economically, scholarships offered provide some variety, but most students are from middle- to upper-middle-class homes. Location-wise, they hail from all 50 states and over 100 foreign countries, and AU prides itself on the booming international student population.

However, a majority of students are white, and some say they expected to see more minority students on campus. Considering how culturally and racially diverse DC is, AU is not a great reflection of that. There are many gay students, which creates a comfortable and accepting atmosphere, as well as many from the northeastern United States.

The College Prowler® Grade on

Diversity: B

A high grade in Diversity indicates that ethnic minorities and international students have a notable presence on campus and that students of different economic backgrounds, religious beliefs, and sexual preferences are well-represented.

Guys & Girls

The Lowdown On...
Guys & Girls

Female Undergrads
61%

Male Undergrads
39%

Birth Control Available?

Yes: Birth control is easily available on campus. Prescriptions for pills and other methods can be obtained from the Student Health Center with an appointment. Other contraceptives are provided across the campus during the year.

Social Scene

The social scene at AU is varied—there's something for everyone. However, AU has an overwhelming female population. Therefore, many of the more attractive young women on campus either lower their standards—looks-wise—or choose to head off-campus to find an equally attractive male counterpart. Ladies, do not fear, though—DC is full of eligible bachelors. Be sure to check out the frat and house parties, clubs, bars, and shows in the area.

Hookups or Relationships?

Both hookups and relationships exist commonly at AU, and both can be obtained if interested. Many of the busiest students opt for hookups though, so as not to interfere with their schoolwork or internships.

Dress Code

Because AU is in the highly-professional capital city, the dress is more formal than most places. Students are often seen wearing suits coming and going from internships or jobs, while slacks and collared shirts are not unusual. Outside of the professional aspect of the fashion at AU, the students are indistinguishable from any other college students. Hoodies and flip-flops are everywhere!

Did You Know?

Top Three Places to Find Hotties:
1. Clubs like Nation and Platinum
2. Bars and restaurants in popular neighborhoods like Adams Morgan
3. Your own dorm

Top Five Places to Hook Up:
1. The amphitheater
2. Courtyard between Hughes and McDowell
3. The stairwells in dorms
4. Davenport Lounge
5. Your own dorm room

Q People Are Average

Most students at American are average in every arena with the exception of politics, where they really shine, in terms of both knowledge and involvement.

Q Looks Are Average

In general, looks are not a main focus at American. Most students are of average attractiveness, and students are usually dressed comfortably, or dressed professionally (i.e. suits, dresses, etc.). AU has a fairly high gay population, and a significant percentage of the student body is in a relationship. Because of this, the population of straight, single students is rather limited.

Q Interesting Mix

The girls are very concerned with appearances for the most part. Most girls, even with an 8:30am class, will come with hair and make up done, skirts and cute tops, and look all nice. A handful, especially the girls on sports teams with early morning practice, come in flip flops and sweats. But it seems like it's only acceptable for those girls to dress like that. There doesn't appear to really be a casual appearance here. The guys are mostly gay, geeky, WAY into partying, or some combo of that. There is a high number of gay students, so dating isn't really an option. The geeky guys are super nice, but definitely very geeky. And have fun, but be wary, of the partying guys.

Q Guys

There are four types of guys at American- gay, jerk, very awkward, or perfect but has a girlfriend.

Q   Arrogant...

Over-dressed for class most of the time (says mid-westerner). Most people are upper-middle class and thus rather arrogant, but you get used to it. SO MANY GAY/QUEER/ALLY/FEMINIST ACTIVISTS!

Q   Student population is really liberal

The student population is really liberal, but in a school that is 60% female and gay friendly, sorry ladies but the outlook for getting a guy here isn't so good.

Q   Boys Are Either...

A. gayB. obsessed with sexC. or never kissed a girl in their lives...So overall, not much to choose from.

Q   Even though there are countless girls, very few of them are attractive.. VERY few.. and there are practically NO "hotties".

The College Prowler Take On...
Guys & Girls

Fear not: you don't have to look like a supermodel to find a mate at AU. The cosmopolitan and ambitious student body tends to place a greater emphasis on individuality, motivation, and intelligence than on appearance, but a fresh, clean-cut look doesn't hurt either.

Straight women at AU complain that satisfactory boyfriends are hard to find, as girls vastly outnumber the guys on campus. Plus, there is a notable gay population. Exploring the greater city may be a more efficient way to hook up. Don't be afraid to go out and meet people at bars, clubs, city organizations, or just on the street.

The College Prowler®
Grade on

Guys & Girls

A high grade for Guys or Girls indicates that the students on campus is attractive, smart, friendly, and engaging, and that the school has a decent gender ratio.

Athletics

The Lowdown On... Athletics

Athletic Association
NAA
NCAA

Athletic Division
NCAA Division I-AAA

Athletic Conferences
Football: N/A
Basketball: Patriot League

School Colors
Red, white, and blue

School Nickname/ Mascot
Eagle

Men Playing Varsity Sports
102: 5%

Women Playing Varsity Sports
141: 4%

Men's Varsity Sports

Basketball
Soccer
Swimming and diving
Track and field
Wrestling

Women's Varsity Sports

Basketball
Field hockey
Lacrosse
Soccer
Swimming and diving
Track and field
Volleyball

Intramurals

Arena baseball
Basketball
Bench press competition
Capture the Flag
Flag football
Sand volleyball
Soccer (indoor, outdoor)
Softball
Tennis
Volleyball

Club Sports

Baseball
Crew
Cricket
Cycling
Equestrian
Field hockey
Gymnastics
Ice Hockey (men's and women's)
Lacrosse (men's and women's)
Rugby (men's and women's)
Sailing
Soccer (men's and women's)
Softball (women's)
Taekwondo
Tennis
Ultimate Frisbee (men's and women's)
Volleyball (women's)

Athletic Fields & Facilities

American Outdoor Tennis Courts
Bender Arena
Reeves Aquatic Center
Reeves Athletic Complex and Greenberg Track
William I. Jacobs Recreational Complex

Most Popular Sports

Basketball, volleyball, and soccer.

Most Overlooked Teams

The wrestling team is well funded, well recruited, and is coached by former Olympians.

School Spirit

The Blue Crew is an increasingly large group of rabid fans that go to sports games covered in team colors that raise a ruckus. Think customized T-shirts, face paint, and wiled crazy cheers.

Getting Tickets

Tickets for events are free to students, though the most popular games fill up fast.

Best Place to Take a Walk

Rock Creek Park, the Nebraska Avenue dog park

Athletics

Q Athletics

The athletic scene is not huge at American. The school spirit is there if you want it but not overwhelming, its no penn state or maryland when it comes to that. The athletic facilities are nice.

Q Decent

School spirit kicks in for the bigger basketball games.

Q Not a Major Focus, but Fun in Its Own Way.

I came from a big football area, and coming to AU was a bit of a shock. The average student cares very little about AU sports, but there are a few shining exceptions, most notably the basketball games: they're free, usually have free food for students, and are well-attended by Greeks and the pep band. AU tries to get everyone excited with different events and giveaways, but the majority of students would rather go off-campus for fun.

Q Mixed Bag

We don't have a football team. Our school instead rallies around our DI basketball team, but it really only sells out during our two biggest traditional days. Club Sports are very popular though, and some are just as if not more competitive than their varsity counterparts. Intramurals, especially among Greek Life, are very popular as well.

Q Sports Not Huge Factor

Sports are not a major part of the scene at American, though the men's basketball team and women's volleyball team have, at times, done well. But if you want to play just for fun, the variety of club and intramural sports is decent. The joke is that politics is the biggest sport on campus.

Q Sports Are Lacking

Varsity sports at American University are lacking. We dont have a football team, tennis team, baseball team. We dont have much school spirit or fan support except for basketball games, and even there it is lacking. Sadly, are athletic department is very poor.

Q Not Very Big

Hardly anyone at American is interested in sports or attending any sort of athletic functions. The majority of students here are either gay or female.

Q

Varsity sports are pretty much a joke. American University (infamously) does not have a football team. The Division I men's basketball team is fun to watch and made the NCAA Tournament for the first time in its history. But in addition to football, there is no varsity team for hockey, baseball, and men's lacrosse.

The College Prowler Take On...
Athletics

AU isn't exactly known for its school spirit. Though the sports teams are Division I, and there are ample intramural teams, many students are less enthused about going to games than going out into DC. Many of the bigger sports fans on campus complain about the absence of a football team—they claim that this contributes to the lack of school spirit on campus.

Some students are trying to get their peers more excited—a recently founded club, the Blue Crew, go all out at the games, painting their faces, and coming up with their own cheers. Basketball and volleyball are popular sports, and in the rare instance where a game is being televised, the turnout is better than usual.

The College Prowler® Grade on

Athletics: C-

A high grade in Athletics indicates that students have school spirit, that sports programs are respected, that games are well-attended, and that intramurals are a prominent part of student life.

Nightlife

The Lowdown On...
Nightlife

Cheapest Place to Get a Drink
Recessions

Primary Areas with Nightlife
Adams Morgan
Dupont Circle
U Street

Closing Time
2 a.m.

Useful Resources for Nightlife
www.washingtonpost.com/
gog

Club Listings

FUR
33 Patterson St. NE
(202) 842-3401
www.furnightclub.com
Open Friday and Saturday,
FUR has three rooms—the
main room or the arena,
a martini lounge, a mafia
room, and the mink lounge.
Thursdays host all types of
music, Fridays are ladies
nights—ladies are admitted
for free (18-or-older for
females, 21-or-older for
males), and host hip hop,
house, international, and latin
rhythms. Saturday hosts a
different DJ in all four rooms,
and tickets may be sold in
advance, sometimes costing
$20. Dress sophisticated and
chic—there is a dress code.

Love
1350 Okie St. NE
(202) 636-9030
www.lovetheclub.com
Music at Love is international,
hip hop, and dance; dress
is upscale; and it features
several levels, a diverse
crowd, and often has theme
nights throughout the week.
Check out its Web site. The
cover varies, and it is 21-and-
over.

Bar Listings

9:30 Club
815 V St. NW
(202) 265-0930
www.930.com
The 9:30 Club is one of
the best venues around to
see some of the biggest
and up-and-coming artists
perform.

Apex
1415 22nd St. NW
(202) 296-0505
www.apex-dc.com
Located in Dupont Circle,
Apex is a popular destination
among AU students. The club
is the longest running gay
dance in the District.

Asylum
2471 18 St. NW
(202) 319-9353
www.asylumdc.com
Asylum features industrial/
metal music, cheap beer,
great burgers and fries.

The Brickskeller
1523 22 St. NW
(202) 293-1885
www.lovethebeer.com
The Brick offers more than
1,000 varieties of beer.

Hawk and Dove
329 Pennsylvania Ave. SE
(202) 543-3300
*www.hawkanddoveonline.
com*

Attracts Capitol Hill staffers and military types; H&D has six rooms, a dance floor, and late-night breakfast and food specials.

Heaven and Hell

2327 18 St. NW
(202) 667-4355
www.clubheavenandhelldc.com
A popular college dance spot, Heaven has an '80's night and techno music, and Hell has a more low-key bar scene with theme drinks like the red-hot 666 shot.

The Improv

1140 Connecticut Ave. NW
(202) 296-7008
www.dcimprov.com
The Improv has stand-up comedy acts that attract big name stars to perform—popular with college students and young people, with lots of good appetizers and a two-drink minimum.

Madam's Organ

2461 18 St. NW
(202) 667-5370
www.madamsorgan.com
One of Adams Morgan's most popular bars, Madam's serves cheap drinks, food, pool tables, a hip, laid-back attitude, and has live music seven nights a week.

Marx Café

3203 Mount Pleasant St. NW
(202) 518-7600
marxcafemtp.com
This spot attracts young hipsters with its communist décor, reggae, Spanish rock music, and great tapas.

Pure Lounge

1326 U St. NW
(202) 667-6680
www.pureloungedc.com

Recessions

1823 L St. NW
(202) 296-6686
www.recessionsdc.com
Recessions is a very cheap downtown bar in the basement of the Commerce building—a great after-work spot. Features nightly drink specials, and cheap food.

Zanzibar

700 Water St. SW
(202) 554-9100
www.zanzibar-otw.com
This is a glamorous bar on DC's waterfront, with exotic food and drinks (African and Caribbean). Zanz also has the best views of the Potomac River—three levels, two VIP lounges, and two sprawling outdoor decks.

Other Places to Check Out

18th Street Lounge
Barking Dog
Black Cat
Bravo
Front Page
Malt Shoppe
Mouse Trap
Nanny O'Brien's
Prince's
Round Table
The Zoo

Favorite Drinking Games

Beer pong
Card games (A$$hole)
Century Club
Power Hour
Quarters

What to Do if You're Not 21

Many bars and clubs, especially in Dupont Circle, are 18-and-up, so even younger students can have a good time out in the city. The Comedy Clubs are also all open to the under-21 crowd.

Organization Parties

Fraternity and sorority parties make up much of the scene for underclassmen, but they are not the iconic frat parties of the movies. AU organizations don't have houses, and the most organized may only have a floor in a residence hall. Parties are held off campus in private houses.

Nightlife

Q Good Once You're Off Campus...

The school tries to put on a lot of events during the weekend to keep people out of trouble, since this is a dry campus, but I'm not sure how much that works. Be sure to go to any oncampus concerts though! I saw some of my favorite bands here for free. The rule here is no alcohol oncampus even if you're 21 and over. However, should you really want to party, there are plenty of frat houses in the area that are usually doing something. And don't forget, this is DC so there are PLENTY of good clubs and dance halls to go to. Take advantage of the city!

Q Frat

House parties, especially frat oriented ones, are ridiculous. They are so much fun and are much safer than traveling into the city.

Q American University Nightlife

DC is a blast, but this is a school for serious students, parties and nightlife are secondary.

Q Eh

Options typically include frat parties and 18 and under nights at clubs for students under 21. Frat parties are most weekends, but weekends do occur where there are none. They're nothing to be compared with frat parties at big state schools, but they are occasionally fun, especially if you're a freshman. In order to go to them you need to wait for rides from sober brothers on campus, which are limited and you're definitely too old for after sophomore, maybe even freshman year. Girls, don't expect to find an abundant amount of attractive males when your out at an AU party.

The clubs in DC are nice if you're into that kind of thing, but if you're more into house parties and such things that occur around campus, AU's not your best bet. Once you are able to get into them, there is an abundance of bars in DC.

Q Nightlife

If you are looking for a party there are only two options. Hang out with friends at the dorms or hang out at a frat party

Q Under 21? Join a Frat!

AU is situated in a pretty suburban, yuppie area of DC, so the nightlife is pretty much frat/house party based. Parties in the dorms are common, but its a dry campus, so you have to be smart about it. If you're looking for more of a club/bar scene you'll have to get on the metro or grab a bus to Adams Morgan or Dupont.

Q

Some of the clubs are MCCXXIII, Dream, Nation, and Insomnia. Bars are a different story. There are countless numbers of bars here. Just take a bus downtown or to Georgetown, and you will find enough bars to drink yourself into   oblivion.

Q

Number one on the list is the 18th Street Lounge. They don't advertise and there's no sign on the door, so you'll have to find someone to take you there. They actually own a record label, and there's usually live music some evenings. It's one of the hottest spots, in my estimation. It's also in the Dupont Circle area, near several other interesting places.

The College Prowler Take On...
Nightlife

DC nightlife is active and exciting enough to wear the most energetic students out. Students will never run out of places to explore when it comes to clubbing and bar hopping. The most interesting places require only a short Metro ride, though there are some spots in Tenleytown for AU students. Clubs will usually admit 18-year-olds, but IDs are carefully checked.

Those who aren't big on dancing and drinking can keep themselves amused, too. Movie theaters, comedy clubs, shows, and concerts abound, as do restaurants and coffeehouses. You won't go bored here.

The College Prowler® Grade on

Nightlife: B+

A high grade in Nightlife indicates that there are many bars and clubs in the area that are easily accessible and affordable. Other determining factors include the number of options for the under-21 crowd and the prevalence of house parties.

Greek Life

The Lowdown On...
Greek Life

Undergrad Men in Fraternities
14%

Undergrad Women in Sororities
16%

Number of Fraternities
12

Number of Sororities
11

Fraternities
Alpha Epsilon Pi
Alpha Sigma Phi
Delta Chi
Delta Tau Delta
Kappa Alpha Psi
Phi Beta Sigma
Phi Sigma Kappa
Pi Kappa Alpha
Pi Kappa Phi
Sigma Chi
Sigma Phi Epsilon
Tau Kappa Epsilon (Colony)

Sororities
Alpha Chi Omega
Alpha Epsilon Phi
Alpha Kappa Alpha
Alpha Nu Omega
Chi Omega
Delta Gamma
Delta Sigma Theta
Lambda Pi Chi
Phi Mu
Phi Sigma Sigma
Zeta Phi Beta

Other Greek Organizations
Greek Council
Greek Peer Advisors
Interfraternity Council
Order of Omega
Panhellenic Council

Greek Life

◯ Bigger Than Their Numbers Give Them Credit.

Greek Life here, though the percentage of students involved may be small, is extremely active during the school year. Welcome week revolves around fraternity parties, and chances are you will go to one within your first week at school. Sororities pride themselves on their annual charity fundraisers and many members of Greek Life are also members of Student Government, the Student Union Board, and other extracurriculars.

◯ Greek Life at AU

There are many different fraternities/sororities to join at AU. If you do not join, however, it is not a school where Greek life students do not associate themselves with non-Greek students. Greek housing is located off campus in nearby Tenleytown. There are also a few professional fraternities. I am in the process of joining a professional fraternity, and I feel they are extremely beneficial to enhance social and academic life.

◯ A Presence, but Not Overwhelmingly So.

I definitely am not the traditional Greek type, but I gave it a try in my second year of school, and it changed my experience at AU for the better. Here's the truth: you can have a fun, social time as a non-Greek at AU, and not in a half-hearted way. But the Greeks are more open here than at other schools, and are generally a fun group that you'll see in your classes and other activities, and it's a genuinely great way to meet new people. If you can bring yourself to pledge, I've found that it's a worthwhile experience.

Okay Greek Life

It is easy to be social and not involved in greek life. However, because the campus is dry, a lot of night life exists because of Greek Life. It is not a large part of campus, at about 25%, but visibly present. Obviously, no Greek houses.

Greek Life Is There If You Want It

It doesn't dominate the social scene but it does play a big role in terms of parties and stuff. It really is what you make it. Personally, I don't enjoy Greek social life so it's been pretty easy for me to avoid it especially with the nightlife alternatives that Washington, DC has to offer.

Avoidable but Worth Checking Out

Greek life definitely has an important role in the party scene, but aside from that it is just like any other student organization on campus. You notice it but if you don't want to be a part of it that is not a big deal. Frats and sororities don't have traditional housing, instead a group of 5 or 6 guys from the same frat will live together and that's where they have parties. I would suggest going to at least one or two parties, because if nothing else it's a good way to meet people.

Greek Life: Fun but Not Vital

Greek life at AU may seem like it's everywhere, but it's really only about 17 to 20 percent of the student body. Parties are fun when you first get to school and want to meet lots of people, but most upperclassmen do apartment/house parties and bars and clubs much more than frat parties. Greek life is also pretty involved in philanthropy, so any event you plan will get a boost from inviting fraternities and sororities.

$\bigcirc$ Greek life isn't a big deal. There are frats and sororities, but they definitely don't dominate the social scene. It's one of those things where you can definitely join if you want, but there isn't any pressure.

The College Prowler Take On...
Greek Life

Students interested in Greek life have plenty of options as to which fraternities and sororities to join, although there are no houses for them on campus. Frats and sororities are a good choice for people who feel overwhelmed and want a surefire way to make friends. Students who don't care about Greek life need not worry, as it is entirely possible to ignore.

Many of the students involved in Greek life live on the noisier south side of campus and are responsible for the rowdy environment there. This makes them easily recognizable for anyone who wants to join in their activities—or anyone who wishes to avoid them like the plague.

The College Prowler® Grade on

Greek Life: B+

A high grade in Greek Life indicates that sororities and fraternities are not only present, but also active on campus. Other determining factors include the variety of houses available and the respect the Greek community receives from the rest of the campus.

Drug Scene

The Lowdown On...
Drug Scene

Most Popular Drugs
Adderall
Alcohol
Marijuana

Alcohol-Related Referrals
244

Alcohol-Related Arrests
0

Drug-Related Referrals
5

Drug-Related Arrests
2

Drug Counseling Programs
American University Health Center
Counseling, workshops, information on drug/alcohol usage, contacts to DC area programs

Drug Scene

Q Party Scene

Its not crazy bad at American. It is there if you go find it but I have never felt pressured by other students. The school is pretty strict.

Q "Officially" a Dry Campus

American University has a dry campus, but obviously that is impossible to enforce. People drink and smoke in the dorms, but it is pretty concealed. Basically everyone goes off campus to drink, smoke, and whatever. I think drinking and smoking has the same popularity.

Q Hardly Any Drugs

As far as I know, there are not many drugs on campus. I have never seen any, but since I dont hang around with that crowd I dont know for sure. There is no peer pressure among most of the students I have met and the campus enforcement seems to be pretty good.

Q Typical College Experience

I definitely don't feel any pressure to drink or do drugs on campus, but I would have to say both drinking and smoking pot are pretty common. You can find some harder drugs if you really want them, but they're not hugely popular. Overall, if you're not blatant with your usage you will be left alone.

Q Hidden Presence

AU is a dry campus, which means no alcohol on campus, even if you're 21. That doesn't mean people don't drink here, it just means they go off campus, or if they're doing it here they do it a little more quietly. Alcohol and weed are present, but avoidable.

Q I Suppose This Is a Good Grade

(CP's grading scale is reversed in my opinion)Underage drinking is virtually universal among the students here. I would also go to say the large majority of students also smoke pot, or at least have no problem being around those that do. Yet, there is never any pressure to do either. Public Safety's policies on both of these are generally more lax than other schools. A first offense for either will usually result with a slap on the wrist and it's relatively very easy to avoid getting caught.

Q

People smoke weed, but not much else. It keeps for a rather calm setting.

Q

It exists, but it isn't too noticeable. Like alcohol, if you want to find it, you will.

Drug Scene

Though students say there is a large variety of drugs available on campus, ranging from pot to opium, it is easy to avoid them. Drugs are not an integral part of students' social lives at AU, but for those that want them, they are certainly available.

AU has a strict drug policy, confiscating drugs and expelling dealers. While this has not made drugs disappear from campus, it means that students who aren't interested need never be exposed to the drug scene. Students at both ends of the drug-use spectrum can live together peacefully without bothering or interfering with each other.

The College Prowler® Grade on

Drug Scene: C

A high grade in the Drug Scene indicates that drugs are not a noticeable part of campus life; drug use is not visible, and no pressure to use them seems to exist.

Campus Strictness

The Lowdown On...
Campus Strictness

Students Are Most Likely to Get Caught...
Drinking
Smoking

Campus Strictness

Some General Stuff

There's always something going on here at AU; you can find people out and about at all hours.Most things socially speaking are pretty relaxed here: there's no curfew, but there are quiet hours that you can get in trouble for violating.No drugs or alcohol on campus (even if you're over 21), and academic integrity is taken very seriously.

Happy University Life

Logical policies that warranty a decent behavior in the student community

Drugs & Drinking

They seem to be very anti-drugs. Pretty of strict about that. As for drinking, technically it is a dry campus but drinking still goes on. It is college after all. Its one of those things were theres are drugs and drinking if you look for it.

Be smart with dorm drinking

dorm drinking is fun, but the noise level has to be kept at a minimum. i got written up for being in a friends room and in the presence of alcohol, which could have been avoided. yet because there were a lot of drunk people, people acted stupid. they didn't tell my parents, and i argued that i didn't know there was alcohol, and their judicial system was just and listened to everyone's side of the story. now i have to write a 3 page paper on what noise means. just don't be loud if you're going to drink or smoke! and act straight in the dorms, if they see you being a fool you'll get transported and have to pay for the ambulance.

Q Punishments Are Harsh

They are strict about underage drinking and drug abuse.

Q School

The school enforces its rules but they aren't nazis about it. The school work is manageable and there is a lot of help there if you need it. The academic policies are enforced.

Q Reasonable

There are locked closets in dorm rooms which RAs are not supposed to search. That's where people stash liquor. Everyone living on a given floor shares cost of vandalism.

Q

AU is very strict. If you get caught, you are in serious trouble! Yet, the campus is far from being actually "dry"—there is a lot of drinking going on. Every Monday, the police blotter in The Eagle reports how many people were transported to the nearby hospital—usually, there is at least one.

Campus Strictness

The trick to being wild and crazy at AU is to do it quietly. Being an enclosed campus, there is not much that students can get away with without campus security noticing. Also, because they have the right to turn you into campus police for punishment, who you get as an RA can decidedly determine your fate.

Students believe that their campus upholds strict rules and penalties when it comes to keeping everyone in line, and as a dry campus, alcohol is not permitted anywhere on the school grounds, even for those over 21. Several students mention recent drug busts, so be forewarned that the campus is cracking down on any and all illegal activity. The advice from current students: if you must partake in activities that the school forbids, then do it quietly in your room and, odds are, you won't get in trouble.

B+

The College Prowler® Grade on

Campus Strictness: B+

A high Campus Strictness grade implies an overall lenient atmosphere; police and RAs are fairly tolerant, and the administration's rules are flexible.

Parking

The Lowdown On...
Parking

Parking Services
Transportation Services
(202) 885-3111
www.american.edu/finance/ts/index.html

Approximate Parking Permit Cost
$936 per year

Student Parking Lot
Yes: There are student parking lots near all dorms, as well as under Katzen Arts Center.

Freshmen Allowed to Park
Yes

Common Parking Tickets

Failure to properly display parking permit: $10
False registration information: $100
No parking area: $60
Parking in a handicapped zone: $150
Parking in more than one space: $40
Parking in No Parking area: $60
Unauthorized parking: $30

Getting a Parking Permit

Parking permits, while expensive, can easily be obtained through the Public Safety Office. They allow for parking almost everywhere on campus.

Did You Know?

Best Places to Find a Parking Spot
Nebraska parking lot, parking garage, side
streets

Good Luck Getting a Parking Spot Here!
The lots behind the dorms

Students Speak Out On...
Parking

Q Really Don't Need One

Parking permits are expensive for the year, but I've never heard of anyone having trouble getting a spot. Most people I know don't have cars here, and if you don't have one, don't worry. Actually, even if you do have one it might not be worth it. DC traffic is awful and it may be more expensive to have a car in this city than its really worth having one around.

Q Well...It's DC

Permits cost nearly 1,000$, and there is no getting away with not having one. However, because there is a shuttle to metro, most kids do not find a need to have their cars on campus. I know many people with cars just sitting in their driveways at home because they refuse to bring them.

Q For Me, Not Worth It at All.

Unless you're going to use it to get back and forth from home (and even then, really consider if the costs and trouble are worth it), I wouldn't recommend bringing a car. It's DC, after all, and it's expensive and hard to find parking. Public Safety loves to ticket cars parked in incorrect spaces even for the time it take to run an errand, so unless you're willing to shell out for an on-campus space, you're going to end up late to things all the time as you frantically search for parking. Really, consider public transportation.

Q Very Limited Parking

Getting parking at AU requires an incredibly expensive permit, as does parking in DC in general. More likely than not, it's not worth it to bring a car.

Ⓠ Confusing and Costly

While AU's parking is technically cheaper than almost any other lot in the city, their parking regulations are impossible to understand as written on the website. Sometimes if you call a person can explain the rules, but even that doesn't always work. Sometimes it just depends on who you talk to, and policies aren't always consistently applied. Especially frustrating is the neighborhood parking policy, which is not the fault of AU but of the local neighborhoods banding together to ban students from parking on the streets. So even if you're legal to park on DC streets, you're not allowed if you're a student. It's a ridiculous policy, and it never should have been made.And of course, even being cheaper than the rest of the city means that it's just an arm rather than an arm and a leg.

Ⓠ Where Is There Parking Anywhere in DC?

I mean, it's not that parking here is bad, it's just that no one really has a car, so parking really isn't needed unless you live off campus or if you are a professor. But parking generally sucks in DC.

Ⓠ Miserable

Parking is abundant on campus. The one problem: parking passes are astronomically high. AU's reason is apparently to lower the school's overall carbon footprint, but I believe this is the wrong way to go about doing this. Truth be told, a car is not necessary but does lend itself to be extremely convenient. If you park your car on campus (OR off-campus) without an AU parking pass, you WILL be fined (pro ably twice in the same day).

Ⓠ

You have to have a parking permit to park on campus. Most people don't have cars, and in DC you really don't need one. My roommate had a car part of the time, and when we lived on campus with the car, it wasn't a problem to get a permit. When we lived off campus, we would only drive to campus at night after some of the parking restrictions were lifted. It's a self-contained campus with really only one road going through, so it's not like there's 'on-street' parking on campus. There is only some parking around the campus.

The College Prowler Take On...
Parking

Parking in DC and on the AU campus is an expensive hassle. AU doesn't allow first-year students to bring cars to campus, and street parking is difficult to find because of the exclusive nature of the surrounding residential area. Parking permits are expensive, running about $450 a semester, and students need to apply for them way in advance. However, if students do get a permit, they believe it is fairly easy to find a spot in one of the on-campus lots.

Students often walk to nearby bars and restaurants and need cars only if they move off campus. Even then, many use the accessible Metro and take the shuttle back and forth from campus. Basically, because DC offers such extensive and inexpensive public transportation, bringing your own car is pretty unnecessary.

The College Prowler® Grade on

Parking: C-

A high grade in the Parking section indicates that parking is both available and affordable, and that parking enforcement isn't overly severe.

Transportation

The Lowdown On...
Transportation

Best Ways to Get Around Town
Cab
Metro
Metrobus

Campus Shuttle
AU Shuttles
The school runs buses across campus and to the Metro station about ever 20 minutes all day.
Monday—Friday 7 a.m. – 12:30 a.m.

Public Transit
The Metro
(202) 637-7000
www.wmata.com

Best Ways to Get to the Airport
The Metro rail system takes students to both Reagan International and Dulles Airport.

Nearest Airport
BWI Airport

Dulles Airport

Reagan National Airport

Nearest Passenger Bus
Union Station, Greyhound
1005 1st St. NE
(202) 289-5154
www.greyhound.com

Nearest Passenger Train
Union Station, Amtrak
900 2nd St. NE
(202) 906-2199
www.amtrak.com

Transportation

Q Variety of Transportation

It's very easy to get around DC; there's a shuttle from AU to the nearby Tenleytown Metro stop, and there are also bus stops along the "N" route of Metrobuses.

Q Shuttles Are Ok

The shuttles at American run until late at night and you usually don't have to wait more than fifteen minutes for one to pick you up.

Q Convenient

There are multiple free school shuttles that go around campus, to the grocery store, and to the nearest metro stop. Metro is seriously the easiest way to get around the city, and don't be afraid to try the buses, they're really convenient once you get the hang of it. Should you be stranded in teh city, call the school's public safety and they'll send a cab to you and take the cab fee out of your student account, so you're never stuck somewhere.

Q Shuttle, Metro, Buses.

Shuttle takes you to metro, which is the best option to getting around DC. The walk isn't bad either. There are, however, frequently delays on the red line. Easy to get to airports. Shared ride programs available through the AU community, too.

Q Washington DC at Your Doorstep

Shuttle from campus to metro stop could come more frequently but it just fine. From there, you have the whole metro system at your finger tips and all the buses, planes, and trains out of the city you could want!

 Not Too Bad

There isn't actually that much to do in the immediate area so if you want to go out you will pretty much need to take a cab or the metro. I would almost always chose to take the metro because it's easier, cheaper and cab companies are not that reliable. However when it comes to going into Tenleytown the school has a shuttle that runs until 2 in the morning on the weekends and starts really early in the morning. It sometimes takes a while so if you're not opposed to walking it can be easier, but the buses will always be there

 Public Transportation: Frustrating but Doable.

AU is not a city school in the traditional sense--it's not surrounded by busy city streets, but more tree-lined ones in front of massive compounds like Homeland Security and the Japanese Embassy, so the walking you'll do sometimes feels much longer than it really is. The shuttles are unreliable, but still the top choice for getting around... but be prepared to have them whiz by you sometimes. The Metro is okay, but I was much happier when I mastered the bus routes (learn where the 30s and N buses go, and you'll be able to avoid the shuttle and red lines altogether). Biking is sort of rough, since we're in a hilly part of DC. And keep in mind that you should make friends with people who have cars, because sometimes (especially when you live off-campus in an apartment) you just need a car.

 It is so convenient. You won't be disappointed. There is a shuttle on campus that runs every 15 minutes and brings you to the subway and major bus route.

Transportation

Hands down, DC is celebrated by students as one of the easiest cities to get around. The Metro, one of the cleanest and most efficient subway systems in the country, runs through DC and even into parts of Virginia and Maryland. Students at AU praise the Metro for its ease, convenience, and proximity to campus. They are able to visit other neighborhoods and get in, out, and around town both quickly and inexpensively.

The Tenleytown Metro stop is the closest to AU, and a short shuttle ride from campus to the stop links students with the entire DC area. With such an extensive Metro system, public transportation is definitely the preferred method of transportation among American University students.

The College Prowler® Grade on

Transportation: A

A high grade for Transportation indicates that campus buses, public buses, cabs, and rental cars are readily-available and affordable. Other determining factors include proximity to an airport and the necessity of transportation.

Weather

The Lowdown On...
Weather

Temperature Averages
Spring – High: 66 °F
Spring – Low: 46 °F
Summer – High: 86 °F
Summer – Low: 68 °F
Fall – High: 68 °F
Fall – Low: 51 °F
Winter – High: 45 °F
Winter – Low: 30 °F

Precipitation Averages
Spring: 3.40 in.
Summer: 3.41 in.
Fall: 3.35 in.
Winter: 2.96 in.

Weather

Q All 4 Seasons...And the Occasional Snowpocalypse.

Summer is humid and gross, but fall and spring are long and pleasant. Winter is usually short, and it doesn't snow more than a few times...unless there's a blizzard, but AU is overcautious and cancels classes often (not a bad thing, if we're being honest).

Q Different Than the West Coast

I came from a place where it rains a ton, so I don't mind it when that does happen, even though it is much more infrequent than I am used to. My biggest complaint is the humidity in the summer. It's really bad, but aside from that the weather is pretty mild.

Q Very Hot and Very Cold

In summer, it sometimes very hot, like 80°s, but it is not bad. Students can lay down on the grass on campus and enjoy the beautiful weather. In winter, it usually does not have much snow, but in February 2010, it snowed a lot and the school had to cancel for a week. The weather is sometimes unstable but it is sunny most of the time.

Q Snows

Tends to snow a lot during winter which hampers commute to classes

Q Up and Down

The weather is kind of unpredictable. It may rain one day, be sunny the next, and snow the day after that. The fall semester is the best time because everybody stays out on the quad laying out and doing work.

Q **Nothing Out of the Ordinary**
Weather in Washington is forever changing. One week
it will be freezing, the next it will be sweltering--literally.
Thankfully, extreme weather here is pretty rare and it's
never too cold or too hot.

Q **It Varies...**
Late July and August are insufferable, but the dorms are air
conditioned. Falls are amazing. Spring it rains constantly.
Winter is chilly, with little snow.

Q The weather is very mild during winter. Sometimes we
get snow, but not very much. Fall is long and beautiful, as
is spring. August and September are usually quite warm
and humid with temperatures in the 80s and 90s. It rains a
lot in winter.

Weather

DC weather tends to be slightly schizophrenic—hot, humid summers, cool winters with some snow, and springs that can range from warm and pleasant to monsoon-infested. AU students' reactions to the weather depend on what they're normally accustomed to, but most say they like the mild winters and long falls.

Students should bring a wide range of clothes for the varied climate. Umbrellas are a must. As long as you build up a tolerance for some rain and unpredictable weather, you should have no problem exploring the city and sightseeing.

The College Prowler® Grade on

Weather: B-

A high Weather grade designates that temperatures are mild and rarely reach extremes, that the campus tends to be sunny rather than rainy, and that weather is fairly consistent rather than unpredictable.

www.collegeprowler.com

Report Card Summary

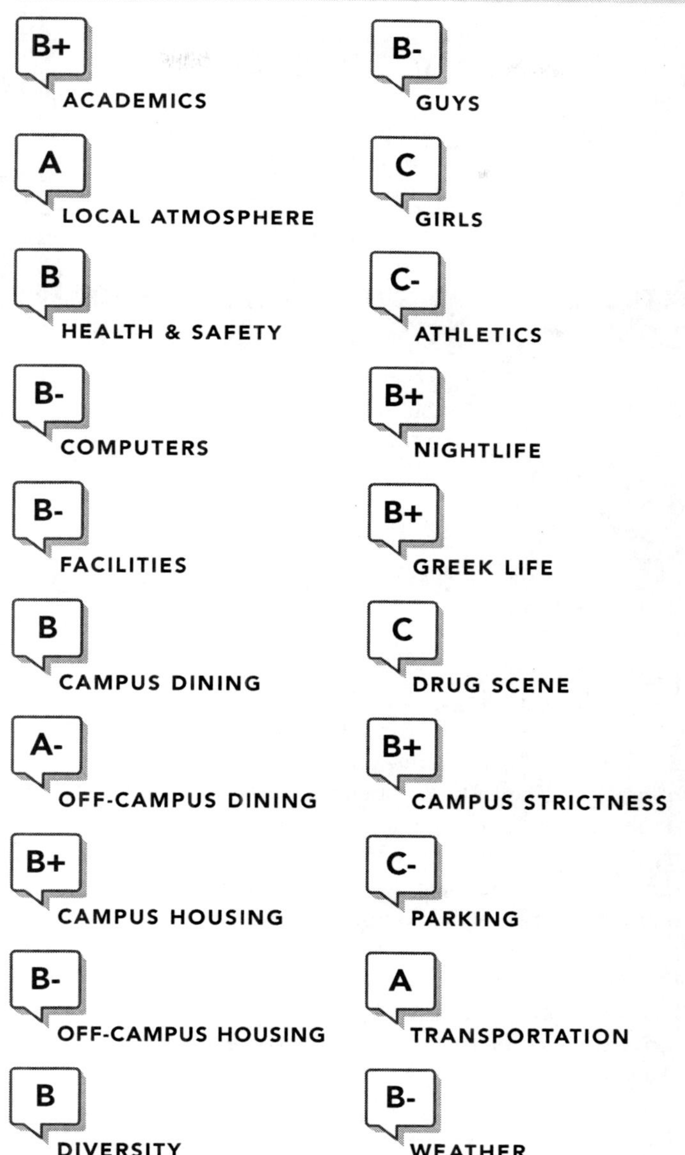

Overall Experience

Students Speak Out On... Overall Experience

A Great College Experience

Located in NW DC, almost in Maryland, the campus has the feeling of being in the suburbs with all the advantages of being in a city. The campus is small enough that you don't get lost, but big enough so that you can always meet new people if you want to. Unlike GW, American University has one main campus focused around a large quad. Freshmen and Sophmores mostly live on campus, and that's great when you're just getting settled in a making friends. By the time you're a Junior or a Senior you have enough friends and understand the city enough to move off-campus and enjoy your independence (and most likely a closer proximity to your internship, job, or favorite nightime spot). Speaking as someone who is graduating in the Spring, I will definitely look back at my years here fondly.

Q AU Is Great

I arrived at AU in a very non-traditional way, but I am extremely happy I ended up here. The size of AU is perfect with roughly 6,000 undergraduates. Some classes are larger than others, but all of my professors are very accommodating and always available for help. Academically speaking, AU is definitely an up-and-coming school. It is becoming much more difficult to get into AU each year. The campus is really pretty, with all the academic building around a common green. The location is fabulous. Downtown DC is a quick metro ride away, and Chevy Chase, MD is within walking distance or one metro stop up and has great restaurants and shopping.

Q Everyone Fits in

I can't be happier with my decision to attend American. There's a place for everyone here. Everyone seems to find their own niche, and the student body is overall pretty friendly.

Q Nice, Small, Expensive; and DC, Politics

The campus is a small, modern, green and beautiful. The professors are nice. AU has an okay or fair variety of courses to choose from. The life quality on campus or around it is pretty high only that it costs some good amount of money. It is an excellent choice if the student is very into politics or international affairs --the academics departments in these fields are very strong and reputed and the location without a doubt is a huge plus --we are right on the Embassy Row. The music and arts, in my opinion, is better than that of other DC universities. AU has a good faculty in this area as well. Having said the above benefits, the general drawbacks would be that the school

and the living cost is expensive and if the student likes
rather bigger study environment/campus, this won't be the
best fit. Oh, the library is PRETTY small as well.

Q Pretty Good

It's right in DC. The school shuttle will take you to the
Metro and from there you can catch the bus or the rail
to ANYWHERE in DC (and some spots in Virginia and
Maryland). It's a great place to see and to experience what
you're learning about in the classroom. There's a place for
everyone. Everyone I know has their group. The professors
are awesome and helpful and care about their students as
more than just a number. It's a kind of unknown college,
but worth it in the end.

Q Great Choice

I chose to come here not entirely sold on it, but knowing
that I wanted to be in DC and at a school that actually had
a campus to hang out on. Since I started coming here I
have fallen more and more in love with the school. The
campus is gorgeous, there's sucha wide range our people
here you're BOUND to make friends no matter what
personality you are, the classes are interesting and the
city is AMAZING. All I can say negative is make sur eyou
check out ratemyprofessor.com before scheduling classes
because who teaches can make all the difference in how
enjoyable aa class is.

Q Overall, Pretty Good

A lot of the facilities are average, including the food. Most
of the teachers are pretty good, however. Overall it's more
academics than parties.

Q Overall Fun

American is a good school for most things, and an
excellent school for very few things. If you're interested in
international relations, it's a good bet, and if you're not,
you should probably look somewhere else.

The College Prowler Take On...
Overall Experience

Many AU students agree that there is something for everyone at their school, and they are rarely ever bored. Though the school's population is relatively small and has fewer parties compared to state schools, many claim that it is worth it for the culture present in DC and the surrounding area.

Upon arrival at AU, the adjustment period can be tough for people not accustomed to an urban setting. However, making friends is quite easy here for even the shyest of students because of the small, tight-knit AU community. Students here, for the most part, have no problems expressing themselves socially or academically. It seems that a "work hard, play hard" philosophy best suits the students at American University.

The Inside Scoop

The Lowdown On...
The Inside Scoop

School Slang
Flaming Cupcake: The flame design protruding from the roof of the Kay Spiritual Center.
Floorcest: Hooking up with someone on your own floor.
JAMed: Getting written up by your RA for various rule violations.
Once an Eagle, Always an Eagle: The slogan for AU alums, especially sports fans.
Sexile: To kick your roomate out so you can hook up.
TDR: Terrace Dining Room— the main cafeteria at AU.

Things I Wish I Knew Before Coming To School
- It's not as small as you think.
- Not reading the newspaper leaves you out of a lot of conversations.

- Owning a suit is a must in DC.
- The city is more than just monuments and museums. Exploration is key.
- The girls-to-guys ratio does make a difference.
- The Metro is super convenient, but it's super expensive, too.

Tips to Succeed
- Extracurriculars are a fantastic way to meet people and build your résumé.
- Get out into the city! You'll make connections and experience an entire metropolis.
- Go to your professors' office hours. The faculty is accessible and available to help you.
- Work on campus, party off campus.

Traditions
Around finals time, students gather in the courtyard between Hughes and McDowell Halls to yell their heads off for Primal Scream and watch other students flash them from the overlooking dorms. It's a stress reliever.

Urban Legends
- A giant mutant beaver-type creature prowls the campus at night.
- An old woman who lived near campus donated a huge sum of money before her death for the perpetual garden maintenance that goes on.
- The black squirrels and gray squirrels that live on campus constantly fight each other.

The Inside Scoop

ℚ AU Means Activism

Though AU rarely markets itself this way, the activism at our school is phenomenal. Everyone has their cause, and everyone is working to save the world in one way or another. There are clubs for everything, and there's an impossibly active branch of Alpha Phi Omega, a co-ed community service fraternity, on campus.

ℚ Plugged-In

At AU, you can be constantly plugged in to what's actually happening in the world, through your classes and outside of them. Students just actually want to do things with their time - Student Government, internships, club sports, theme parties. We send one of the highest percentages of our students to the Peace Corps compared to other schools. We have crazy high numbers of Boren Scholarship recipients (paid by the State Department to study abroad for a year, and get a guaranteed job on graduation). Our Career Center is phenomenal; they will get you where you want to be, whether in DC or anywhere else. I have had 3 internships in 3 years, and got academic credit for all of them, plus support and guidance from professors in the fields I was exploring. The vast majority of us will study abroad. My professors actually work in the fields they teach, from accounting to diplomacy to budget policy. DC is my classroom. Basically, I feel like we experience and debate the news before the rest of the world has time to refresh the New York Times homepage.

ℚ Internships Rule All

I transferred to AU because I had a panic attack sophomore year about not being able to find a job post-graduation. Everyone I've talked to has a serious preference towards

AU grads because they tend to be less entitled and work harder than the other schools in DC. I've had four internships since I transferred here, and I know that it'll be the difference between me and kids at my old school who only babysat for four years.

Q Things to Be Proud

Excellent teachers staff, great location, lot of opportunities to learn and grow

Q Good Quality Academics, Superior International Affairs and Political Science, and DC

The facilities are pretty modern. I think they are pretty good in general. The library is small, although students have access to a greater variety of resources though interlibrary loan, library's subscription to online databases and the Library of Congress.Academic programs are in general of good --and fairly reputed nationally-- quality. International Studies as well as Political Science are the two biggest, best and most well known programs, but other disciplines are fair as well. Just that because AU is a small private school some departments less related to politics/international affairs can get pretty small --like physics. Unique opportunities would definitely be the political scene in DC. Lots of events, conferences, demonstrations, embassy events, etc. AU gets ambassadors and other US and foreign government officials as well as non-government workers to speak at the school quite often. Internships available during academic semesters as well as during summer are another big, big plus.

Q Go American!

One of the many reasons I chose to attend this school is the diversity. American's Study Abroad program is one of the best in the country with 30+ different places to study. I would highly recommend this school to anyone who wants to travel! The social scene is also extremely diverse. The Gay & Lesbian community has certainly stepped up their game. 33 percent of the male population is gay. If you are

a white-bred person, you are going to be the minority.
Most of the students are Middle Eastern, Asian, African
American, etc. Since the campus is really small and closely-
knit, you are friends with almost everyone you meet at
events, in the cafeteria's and at clubs. The school in itself
feels like a family.

Serious Academics, Cultural Diversity

Academic programs are really great, especially for
international studies majors. Most people on campus, even
the party animals, are really into what they're studying. The
location is definitely important--even if you don't get off-
campus very often, being in DC gives lots of opportunities.
Racial diversity isn't great, but cultural and experiential
diversity is huge.

LGBTQ, Internships, Study Abroad, Passion About Politics

Internships, study abroad options, peers that want to talk
politics with you, and LGBTQ tolerance and resources
are abundant. You will probably feel a little left out if you
aren't very into politics or if you are not super liberal, but
these things wont have a detrimental effect on your AU
experience.

Jobs & Internships

The Lowdown On...
Jobs & Internships

Career Center

Career Center, Butler Pavilion Room 5th Floor

(202) 885-1804

careercenter@american.edu

www.american.edu/ careercenter

Monday 9 a.m.–5 p.m., Tuesday 9 a.m.– 8 p.m., Wednesday 9 a.m.–8 p.m., Thursday 10 a.m.–5 p.m., Friday 9 a.m.–5 p.m.

Employment Services?

Yes

Placement Services?

No

Other Career Services

Interview preparation
Jobs/internship opportunities
Resume and cover letter help

Advice

Make use of the Career Center. Learn how to write professional cover letters and resumes, and keep your eyes opened for fliers posted around campus offering positions. Surf the Internet for opportunities, and form relationships with your professors so they can write you recommendations or give you advice on where to apply. Be careful about your Facebook page and what you make public, because most employers in DC check them before hiring.

Firms That Most Frequently Hire Grads

Clear Channel Radio
Deloitte and Touche LLP
International Center for Research on Women
National Institutes of Health
Peace Corps
Teach for America
U.S. Department of Justice
U.S. Department of State

Alumni & Post-Grads

The Lowdown On...
Alumni & Post-Grads

Alumni Office
Office of Development
4400 Massachusetts Ave.
NW, Washington, D.C.
Phone: (202) 885-5960
gift@american.edu
alumni.american.edu

Major Alumni Events
Alumni Welcome Back
Homecoming
Travel opportunities

Services Available
Alumni career services
AU store discounts
Insurance
National chapters

Alumni Publications
Alumni Association
Newsletter

Did You Know?

Famous AU Alumni:
Robert Byrd (Class of '63) – Senator (D-WV)
Judith Sheindlin "Judge Judy" (Class of '63) – TV show host
Al Koken (Class of '74) – Talkshow Host, WTEM Sports Talk Radio
Robert Engel (Class of '82) – Executive Director, Committee for an Effective Congress
Goldie Hawn (Incomplete degree) – Actress
Star Jones (Class of '83) – Co-host, The View
David Aldridge (Class of '87) – ESPN analyst
Mike Mills (Class of '88) – Staff Writer, the Washington Post

Student Organizations

The Lowdown On...

ROTC
Air Force ROTC: Yes
Navy ROTC: Yes
Army ROTC: Yes

Student Activities Offered

Academic Affairs
Accounting Club
Active Minds at AU
African Students'
Organization
Alliance of Students Against
Poverty
American Marketing
Association
American Medical Student
Association
American Student Peace
Alliance
American Television
American Word
Amnesty International
Anime Society
Arabic Club
Arts Council
Asian MBA Association
Association of Computing
Machinery
AU Players
AU Students for Liberty
Balkan Beats
Ballroom Dancing
Baptist Student Association
Black MBA Association
Black Student Alliance
Brazilian Club
British Society
Bull Moose Party
Caribbean Circle
Catholic Student Association
Chi Alpha Christian
Fellowship
Chinese Language Club
Chinese Students and
Scholars Association
Circus Club
Clocks & Clouds: The
American University
Undergraduate Research
Journal
Club Bulgaria
College Democrats
College Republicans
Colleges Against Cancer
Community Action and Social
Justice Coalition
Creative Peace Initiatives
Creative Writing Club
D.C. Today D.C. Tomorrow
Debate Society
Dime a Dozen (coed a
cappella group)
Dinosaurs Against Fossil
Fuels
The Eagle (campus
newspaper)
Eco-Sense
Entrepreneurs Club
Event Planning and Catering
Club
Exploring the D.C. Art World
Facilitating Leadership in
Youth (FLY)
Film Society
Gamers
German Club
Gospel Choir
Habitat for Humanity
Hispanic Business Association
International Development
Program
InterVarsity Graduate
Christian Fellowship
Italian Club

Japanese Student
Association
Jewish Student Association
Justice Not Jails
Kogod Real Estate Club
Korean Student Association
Latino and American Student
Organization
Martial Arts Organization
Math Club
Middle East and North Africa
Students' Association
Mission: Improv-able
Model United Nations
Movement for Global Justice
Muslim Student Association
NAACP
National Coalition to Abolish
the Death Penalty
Objectivist Society
Outdoors Club
Patriots for Peace
Persian Club
Pre-Health Society
Queers and Allies
Quizbowl
Rationalists and Atheists
Relay for Life Club
Rock On! (rock-climbing club)
Russian Club
Science Fiction and Fantasy
Club
Solidarity
Southern Love
Spinoza Practice Club
Step 101
Student Government
Students for Choice
Students for Justice in
Palestine

Students for Sensible Drug
Policy
Taiwanese Student
Association
Teach for America
Thai Student Association
Turkish American Students
Association
Undergraduate Business
Association
Unitarian Universalists, AU
United Methodist Student
Association
University Diversity
Vietnamese Student
Association
Women's Initiative
Youth for Western Civilization

The Best

The BEST Things

1. Small classes

2. Politically passionate students and faculty

3. Great food off campus

4. Internship opportunities in the city

5. Comfortable, clean, and friendly dorms

6. Large international student population

7. Small campus

8. The Career Center

9. AU Abroad program for studying internationally

10. Engaging and expert professors

The Worst

The WORST Things

1. Administrative bureaucracy

2. Expensive tuition

3. Very limited math program

4. Cost of living

5. Overwhelming political focus of the campus

6. Weak programs for the hard sciences

7. Limited course selection in smaller departments

8. The unbalanced female-to-male ratio

9. Dry campus

10. Student cliques

The Lowdown On...
Visiting

Campus Tours
Visit AU's Web site for dates and times of tours and information sessions, or if you have any questions, please call admissions at (202) 885-6000.

Virtual Tour of Campus
www.american.edu/tour

Interviews & Information Sessions
Contact the tours and information offices at (202) 885-6000 or e-mail afa@american.edu

Overnight Visits

Regular overnights, and special Honors overnights available.
Orientations required for all incoming freshman in the summer.
Separate orientation for international students.

Words to Know

Academic Probation – A suspension imposed on a student if he or she fails to keep up with the school's minimum academic requirements. Those unable to improve their grades after receiving this warning can face dismissal.

Beer Pong/Beirut – A drinking game involving cups of beer arranged in a pyramid shape on each side of a table. The goal is to get a ping pong ball into one of the opponent's cups by throwing the ball or hitting it with a paddle. If the ball lands in a cup, the opponent is required to drink the beer.

Bid – An invitation from a fraternity or sorority to 'pledge' (join) that specific house.

Blue-Light Phone – Brightly-colored phone posts with a blue light bulb on top. These phones exist for security purposes and are located at various outside locations around most campuses. In an emergency, a student can pick up one of these phones (free of charge) to connect with campus police or a security escort.

Campus Police – Police who are specifically assigned to a given institution. Campus police are typically not regular city officers; they are employed by the university in a full-time capacity.

Club Sports – A level of sports that falls somewhere between varsity and intramural. If a student is unable to commit to a varsity team but has a lot of passion for athletics, a club sport could be a better, less intense option. Even less demanding, intramural (IM) sports often involve no traveling and considerably less time.

Cocaine – An illegal drug. Also known as "coke" or "blow," cocaine often resembles a white crystalline or powdery substance. It is highly addictive and dangerous.

Common Application – An application with which students can apply to multiple schools.

Course Registration – The period of official class selection for the upcoming quarter or semester. Prior to registration, it is best to prepare several back-up courses in case a particular class becomes full. If a course is full, students can place themselves on the waitlist, although this still does not guarantee entry.

Division Athletics – Athletic classifications range from Division I to Division III. Division IA is the most competitive, while Division III is considered to be the least competitive.

Dorm – A dorm (or dormitory) is an on-campus housing facility. Dorms can provide a range of options from suite-style rooms to more communal options that include shared bathrooms. Most first-year students live in dorms. Some upperclassmen who wish to stay on campus also choose this option.

Early Action – An application option with which a student can apply to a school and receive an early acceptance response without a binding commitment. This system is becoming less and less available.

Early Decision – An application option that students should use only if they are certain they plan to attend the school in question. If a student applies using the early decision option and is admitted, he or she is required and bound to attend that university. Admission rates are usually higher among students who apply through early decision, as the student is clearly indicating that the school is his or her first choice.

Ecstasy – An illegal drug. Also known as "E" or "X," ecstasy looks like a pill and most resembles an aspirin. Considered a party drug, ecstasy is very dangerous and can be deadly.

Ethernet – An extremely fast Internet connection available in most university-owned residence halls. To use an Ethernet connection properly, a student will need a network card and cable for his or her computer.

Fake ID – A counterfeit identification card that contains false information. Most commonly, students get fake IDs with altered birthdates so that they appear to be older than 21 (and therefore of legal drinking age). Even though it is illegal, many college students have fake IDs in hopes of purchasing alcohol or getting into bars.

Frosh – Slang for "freshman" or "freshmen."

Hazing – Initiation rituals administered by some fraternities or sororities as part of the pledging process. Many universities have outlawed hazing due to its degrading, and sometimes dangerous, nature.

Intramurals (IMs) – A popular, and usually free, sport league in which students create teams and compete against one another. These sports vary in competitiveness and can include a range of activities—everything from billiards to water polo. IM sports are a great way to meet people with similar interests.

Keg – Officially called a half-barrel, a keg contains roughly 200 12-ounce servings of beer.

LSD – An illegal drug, also known as acid, this hallucinogenic drug most commonly resembles a tab of paper.

Marijuana – An illegal drug, also known as weed or pot; along with alcohol, marijuana is one of the most commonly found drugs on campuses across the country.

Major –The focal point of a student's college studies; a specific topic that is studied for a degree. Examples of majors include physics, English, history, computer science, economics, business, and music. Many students decide on a specific major before arriving on campus, while others are simply "undecided" until declaring a major. Those who are extremely interested in two areas can also choose to double major.

Meal Block – The equivalent of one meal. Students on a meal plan usually receive a fixed number of meals per week. Each meal, or "block," can be redeemed at the school's dining facilities in place of cash. Often, a student's weekly allotment of meal blocks will be forfeited if not used.

Minor – An additional focal point in a student's education. Often serving as a complement or addition to a student's main area of focus, a minor has fewer requirements and prerequisites to fulfill than a major. Minors are not required for graduation from most schools; however some students who want to explore many different interests choose to pursue both a major and a minor.

Mushrooms – An illegal drug. Also known as "'shrooms," this drug resembles regular mushrooms but is extremely hallucinogenic.

Off-Campus Housing – Housing from a particular landlord or rental group that is not affiliated with the university. Depending on the college, off-campus housing can range from extremely popular to non-existent. Students who choose to live off campus are typically given more freedom, but they also have to deal with possible subletting scenarios, furniture, bills, and other issues. In addition to these factors, rental prices and distance often affect a student's decision to move off campus.

Office Hours – Time that teachers set aside for students who have questions about coursework. Office hours are a good forum for students to go over any problems and to show interest in the subject material.

Pledging – The early phase of joining a fraternity or sorority, pledging takes place after a student has gone through rush and received a bid. Pledging usually lasts between one and two semesters. Once the pledging period is complete and a particular student has done everything that is required to become a member, that student is considered a brother or sister. If a fraternity or a sorority would decide to "haze" a group of students, this initiation would take place during the pledging period.

Private Institution – A school that does not use tax revenue to subsidize education costs. Private schools typically cost more than public schools and are usually smaller.

Prof – Slang for "professor."

Public Institution – A school that uses tax revenue to subsidize education costs. Public schools are often a good value for in-state residents and tend to be larger than most private colleges.

Quarter System (or Trimester System) – A type of academic calendar system. In this setup, students take classes for three academic periods. The first quarter usually starts in late September or early October and concludes right before Christmas. The second quarter usually starts around early to mid–January and finishes up around March or April. The last academic quarter, or "third quarter," usually starts in late March or early April and finishes up in late May or Mid-June. The fourth quarter is summer. The major difference between the quarter system and semester system is that students take more, less comprehensive courses under the quarter calendar.

RA (Resident Assistant) – A student leader who is assigned to a particular floor in a dormitory in order to help to the other students who live there. An RA's duties include ensuring student safety and providing assistance wherever possible.

Recitation – An extension of a specific course; a review session. Some classes, particularly large lectures, are supplemented with mandatory recitation sessions that provide a relatively personal class setting.

Rolling Admissions – A form of admissions. Most commonly found at public institutions, schools with this type of policy continue to accept students throughout the year until their class sizes are met. For example, some schools begin accepting students as early as December and will continue to do so until April or May.

Room and Board – This figure is typically the combined cost of a university-owned room and a meal plan.

Room Draw/Housing Lottery – A common way to pick on-campus room assignments for the following year. If a student decides to remain in university-owned housing, he or she is assigned a unique number that, along with seniority, is used to determine his or her housing for the next year.

Rush – The period in which students can meet the brothers and sisters of a particular chapter and find out if a given fraternity or sorority is right for them. Rushing a fraternity or a sorority is not a requirement at any school. The goal of rush is to give students who are serious about pledging a feel for what to expect.

Semester System – The most common type of academic calendar system at college campuses. This setup typically includes two semesters in a given school year. The fall semester starts around the end of August or early September and concludes before winter vacation. The spring semester usually starts in mid-January and ends in late April or May.

Student Center/Rec Center/Student Union – A common area on campus that often contains study areas, recreation facilities, and eateries. This building is often a good place to meet up with fellow students; depending on the school, the student center can have a huge role or a non-existent role in campus life.

Student ID – A university-issued photo ID that serves as a student's key to school-related functions. Some schools require students to show these cards in order to get into dorms, libraries, cafeterias, and other facilities. In addition to storing meal plan information, in some cases, a student ID can actually work as a debit card and allow students to purchase things from bookstores or local shops.

Suite – A type of dorm room. Unlike dorms that feature communal bathrooms shared by the entire floor, suites offer bathrooms shared only among the suite. Suite-style dorm rooms can house anywhere from two to ten students.

TA (Teacher's Assistant) – An undergraduate or grad student who helps in some manner with a specific course. In some cases, a TA will teach a class, assist a professor, grade assignments, or conduct office hours.

Undergraduate – A student in the process of studying for his or her bachelor's degree.

About the Author

Name: Ian Hosking

Hometown:

Major:

Fun Fact:

Previous Contributors: Alanna Schubach

Pros and Cons

Still can't figure out if this is the right school for you? You've already read through this in-depth guide; why not list the pros and cons? It will really help with narrowing down your decision and determining whether or not this school is right for you.

Pros	**Cons**
....	....
....	....
....	....
....	....
....	....
....	....
....	....
....	....
....	....
....	....
....	....

Pros and Cons

Still can't figure out if this is the right school for you? You've already read through this in-depth guide; why not list the pros and cons? It will really help with narrowing down your decision and determining whether or not this school is right for you.

Pros	**Cons**
....	....
....	....
....	....
....	....
....	....
....	....
....	....
....	....
....	....
....	....
....	....

Notes

Notes

Notes

Notes

Notes

Notes

Notes

Notes

Notes

Notes

Notes

....

....

....

....

....

....

....

....

....

....

....

....

....

....

Notes

Notes

Notes

Notes

Notes

College Scholarships

Search. Apply. Win!

College Prowler gives away thousands of dollars each month through our popular monthly scholarships, including our $2,000 "No Essay" scholarship.

Plus, we'll connect you with hundreds of other scholarships based on your unique information and qualifications!

Create a College Prowler account today to get matched with millions of dollars in relevant scholarships!

Sign up and apply now at
www.collegeprowler.com/register

Review Your School!

Let your voice be heard.

Every year, thousands of students take our online survey to share their opinions about campus life. 

Now's your chance to help millions of high school students choose the right college for them.

Tell us what life is really like at your school by taking our online survey or even uploading your own photos and videos!

And as our thanks to you for participating in our survey, we'll enter you into a random drawing for our $1,000 Monthly Survey Scholarship!

**For more information, check out
www.collegeprowler.com/survey**

Albion College
Alfred University
Allegheny College
Alverno College
American Intercontinental University Online
American University
Amherst College
Arizona State University
Ashford University
The Art Institute of California – Orange County
Auburn University
Austin College
Babson College
Ball State University
Bard College
Barnard College
Barry University
Baruch College
Bates College
Bay Path College
Baylor University
Beloit College
Bentley University
Berea College
Binghamton University
Birmingham Southern College
Bob Jones University
Boston College
Boston University
Bowdoin College
Bradley University
Brandeis University
Brigham Young University
Brigham Young University – Idaho
Brown University
Bryant University
Bryn Mawr College
Bucknell University
Cal Poly Pomona
California College of the Arts
California Institute of Technology
California Polytechnic State University
California State University – Monterey Bay
California State University – Northridge
California State University – San Marcos
Carleton College
Carnegie Mellon University
Case Western Reserve University
Catawba College
Catholic University of America

Centenary College of Louisiana
Centre College
Chapman University
Chatham University
City College of New York
City College of San Francisco
Claflin University
Claremont McKenna College
Clark Atlanta University
Clark University
Clemson University
Cleveland State University
Colby College
Colgate University
College of Charleston
College of Mount Saint Vincent
College of Notre Dame of Maryland
College of the Holy Cross
College of William & Mary
College of Wooster
Colorado College
Columbia College Chicago
Columbia University
Concordia University – Wisconsin
Connecticut College
Contra Costa College
Cornell College
Cornell University
Creighton University
CUNY Lehman College
CUNY Queens College
CUNY Queensborough Community College
Dalton State College
Dartmouth College
Davidson College
De Anza College
Del Mar College
Denison University
DePaul University
DePauw University
Diablo Valley College
Dickinson College
Dordt College
Drexel University
Duke University
Duquesne University
Earlham College
East Carolina University
Eckerd College
El Paso Community College
Elon University
Emerson College
Emory University
Fashion Institute of Design & Merchandising

Fashion Institute of Technology
Ferris State University
Florida Atlantic University
Florida Southern College
Florida State University
Fordham University
Franklin & Marshall College
Franklin Pierce University
Frederick Community College
Freed-Hardeman University
Furman University
Gannon University
Geneva College
George Mason University
George Washington University
Georgetown University
Georgia Institute of Technology
Georgia Perimeter College
Georgia State University
Germanna Community College
Gettysburg College
Gonzaga University
Goucher College
Grinnell College
Grove City College
Guilford College
Gustavus Adolphus College
Hamilton College
Hampshire College
Hampton University
Hanover College
Harvard University
Harvey Mudd College
Hastings College
Haverford College
Hillsborough Community College
Hofstra University
Hollins University
Howard University
Hunter College (CUNY)
Idaho State University
Illinois State University
Illinois Wesleyan University
Indiana Univ.–Purdue Univ. Indianapolis (IUPUI)
Indiana University
Iowa State University
Ithaca College
Jackson State University
James Madison University
Johns Hopkins University
Juniata College
Kansas State University
Kaplan University

Kent State University
Kenyon College
La Roche College
Lafayette College
Lawrence University
Lehigh University
Lewis & Clark College
Linfield College
Los Angeles City College
Los Angeles Valley College
Louisiana College
Louisiana State University
Loyola College in Maryland
Loyola Marymount University
Loyola University Chicago
Luther College
Macalester College
Macomb Community College
Manhattan College
Manhattanville College
Marlboro College
Marquette University
Maryville University
Massachusetts College of Art & Design
Massachusetts Institute of Technology
McGill University
Merced College
Mercyhurst College
Messiah College
Miami University
Michigan State University
Middle Tennessee State University
Middlebury College
Millsaps College
Minnesota State University – Moorhead
Missouri State University
Montana State University
Montclair State University
Moorpark College
Mount Holyoke College
Muhlenberg College
New College of Florida
New York University
North Carolina A&T State University
North Carolina State University
Northeastern University
Northern Arizona University
Northern Illinois University
Northwest Florida State College
Northwestern College – Saint Paul
Northwestern University

Oakwood University
Oberlin College
Occidental College
Oglethorpe University
Ohio State University
Ohio University
Ohio Wesleyan University
Old Dominion University
Onondaga Community
College
Oral Roberts University
Pace University
Palm Beach State College
Penn State Altoona
Penn State Brandywine
Penn State University
Pepperdine University
Pitzer College
Pomona College
Princeton University
Providence College
Purdue University
Radford University
Ramapo College of
New Jersey
Reed College
Rensselaer Polytechnic
Institute
Rhode Island School
of Design
Rhodes College
Rice University
Rider University
Robert Morris University
Rochester Institute
of Technology
Rocky Mountain College
of Art & Design
Rollins College
Rowan University
Rutgers University
Sacramento State
Saint Francis University
Saint Joseph's University
Saint Leo University
Salem College
Salisbury University
Sam Houston State
University
Samford University
San Diego State University
San Francisco State
University
Santa Clara University
Santa Fe College
Sarah Lawrence College
Scripps College
Seattle University
Seton Hall University
Simmons College
Skidmore College
Slippery Rock University
Smith College

South Texas College
Southern Methodist
University
Southwestern University
Spelman College
St. John's College
– Annapolis
St. John's University
St. Louis University
St. Mary's University
St. Olaf College
Stanford University
State University of New
York – Purchase College
State University of New
York at Fredonia
State University of New
York at Oswego
Stetson University
Stevens-Henager College
Stony Brook University
(SUNY)
Susquehanna University
Swarthmore College
Syracuse University
Taylor University
Temple University
Tennessee State University
Texas A&M University
Texas Christian University
Texas Tech
The Community College
of Baltimore County
Towson University
Trinity College (Conn.)
Trinity University (Texas)
Troy University
Truman State University
Tufts University
Tulane University
Union College
University at Albany
(SUNY)
University at Buffalo
(SUNY)
University of Alabama
University of Arizona
University of Arkansas
University of Arkansas
at Little Rock
University of California
– Berkeley
University of
California – Davis
University of
California – Irvine
University of California
– Los Angeles
University of California
– Merced
University of California
– Riverside
University of California
– San Diego

University of California
– Santa Barbara
University of California
– Santa Cruz
University of Central
Florida
University of Chicago
University of Cincinnati
University of Colorado
University of Connecticut
University of Delaware
University of Denver
University of Florida
University of Georgia
University of Hartford
University of Illinois
University of Illinois
at Chicago
University of Iowa
University of Kansas
University of Kentucky
University of Louisville
University of Maine
University of Maryland
University of Maryland
– Baltimore County
University of
Massachusetts
University of Miami
University of Michigan
University of Minnesota
University of Mississippi
University of Missouri
University of Montana
University of Mount Union
University of Nebraska
University of Nevada
– Las Vegas
University of New
Hampshire
University of North
Carolina
University of North
Carolina – Greensboro
University of Notre Dame
University of Oklahoma
University of Oregon
University of Pennsylvania
University of Phoenix
University of Pittsburgh
University of Puget Sound
University of Rhode Island
University of Richmond
University of Rochester
University of San Diego
University of San Francisco
University of South
Carolina
University of South Dakota
University of South Florida
University of Southern
California
University of St
Thomas – Texas

University of Tampa
University of Tennessee
University of Tennessee
at Chattanooga
University of Texas
University of Utah
University of Vermont
University of Virginia
University of Washington
University of Western
Ontario
University of Wisconsin
University of
Wisconsin – Stout
Urbana University
Ursinus College
Valencia Community
College
Valparaiso University
Vanderbilt University
Vassar College
Villanova University
Virginia Commonwealth
University
Virginia Tech
Virginia Union University
Wagner College
Wake Forest University
Warren Wilson College
Washington &
Jefferson College
Washington & Lee
University
Washington University
in St. Louis
Wellesley College
Wesleyan University
West Los Angeles College
West Point Military
Academy
West Virginia University
Western Illinois University
Western Kentucky
University
Wheaton College (Ill.)
Wheaton College (Mass.)
Whitman College
Wilkes University
Willamette University
Williams College
Xavier University
Yale University
Youngstown State
University

Order now! • *collegeprowler.com* • (800) 290-2682
More than 400 single-school guides available!

CPSIA information can be obtained at www.ICGtesting.com
Printed in the USA
237239LV00001B/1/P